D1461008

HIDDEN KERRY

BREDA JOY

HIDDEN KERRY

THE KEYS TO THE KINGDOM

MERCIER PRESS
IRISH PUBLISHER – IRISH STORY

For my father, Brendan, who tells a good story.

MERCIER PRESS

Cork

www.mercierpress.ie

© Breda Joy, 2014

ISBN: 978 1 78117 220 9

10 9 8 7 6 5 4 3 2 1

A CIP record for this title is available from the British Library

Printed and bound in the EU.

Contents

Acknowledgements

The opportunity to write this book came my way thanks to photographer Valerie O'Sullivan, who told Mary Feehan of Mercier Press that I had a project on hand about Kerry. Mary put me on the road with a job of work which has afforded me immense satisfaction. Most importantly, she set a deadline which gave me, alternately, a sharp focus and bouts of blind panic.

I received an amount of help from James O'Connor, Allman's Terrace, Killarney, who has a burning interest in local history and the outdoors. Another pillar of my research was Dingle parish priest Canon Tomás B. Ó Luanaigh, former president of the Kerry Archaeological and Historical Society, which was also an invaluable resource. Other society members who helped me to source information were Noel Grimes, Killarney, and Isabel Bennett, archaeologist and curator of *Músaem Chorca Dhuibhne* (Dingle Peninsula Museum). I am particularly grateful to Gordon Revington, my colleague in *Kerry's Eye*, for drawing my attention to the Second World War heroine, Janie McCarthy. Gordon directed me to Paris-based Isadore Ryan, another man with a fund of knowledge. My thanks to both writers for filling me in on her heroic work in Paris. The erudite Monsignor Pádraig Ó Fiannachta was only ever an email away to enlighten me, especially on the roots of obscure expressions *as Gaeilge*. I could not have reimagined the

Austen-like existence of the Delap sisters without the primary source material provided by their descendant, Joanna Lee of Dublin. Kenmare historian Gerard Lyne was of immense help.

The material in this book is largely drawn from my forays into the Kerry countryside and from the written word. There was no 'big plan' and serendipity worked its usual magic. My work as a journalist in Kerry for the past twenty-eight years stood me in good stead. This book would have been much the poorer without the 'guides' who shared their knowledge and memories of their own places: Patrick Lynch, Tarbert; Michael Leane, Killarney; Junior Murphy, Cahersiveen; Michael Egan, Valentia Island; Bobby Hanley, Kenmare; Mike O'Donnell and Tomás Slattery, Tralee; Michael Guerin, Listowel; and Bernard Goggin, Dingle. Sadly, Bobby Hanley passed away on Monday 11 August 2014.

Fr Pat Moore introduced me to the Smearlagh Way and Jesse James territory. Thanks also to Peter Malone for providing a list of West Kerry 'leads'. Seán Quinlan of the Rattoo Heritage Society in North Kerry filled out my understanding of his area.

Pádraig and Kerry Kennelly of *Kerry's Eye* eliminated a major headache by formatting the photographs for me. Colleague Bridget McAuliffe gave me sound advice. Jimmy Darcy, sports journalist and colleague, took on 'Brosnan and Sheehy, Peacebrokers', the one essay I judged it wiser to 'sub-contract'.

My research led me to some marvellous books, including Kathleen O'Rourke's *Old Killarney*, kindly loaned to me by Maura O'Sullivan. I re-read Joseph O'Connor's *Hostage to Fortune*, a pure gem. It was reassuring also to have my copy of T. J. Barrington's *Discovering Kerry* at my back when I needed extra

facts. Thank you to Kerry County Librarian Tommy O'Connor
and his Tralee staff, including Michael Lynch, Noirín O'Keeffe
and Tina Cronin; thanks also to Killarney Librarian Éamonn
Browne and his staff, to Cahersiveen Library, and to Patricia
O'Hare and her staff at the Muckross House Research Library.

I owe a debt of gratitude to Eileen Sheehan, Liz O'Brien
and Valerie O'Sullivan for their wise counsel when I was getting
frazzled. Special mention to my aunt, Lily O'Shaughnessy,
for all those 'Muckross dinners'. Last, but not least, a word of
appreciation of my calm son, Brendan, for cooking at weekends
when the only culinary offering in the house was fried brain
(mine).

Finally I would like to thank everyone at my publishers,
Mercier Press, as well as Liz Hudson and Rachel Hutchings for
their invaluable work on the book.

Countless people helped me to gather the stories between
these covers. It is impossible to thank everyone individually, but
if I have left anyone significant out, please put it down to one
of my 'senior moments'; believe me, there are many. I deeply
appreciate everyone's help and hope to return it in kind where
possible. *Ar scáth a chéile a mhairmíd*: We all live in the shelter
of one another.

Introduction

'Do I not meet scores of people who tell me they would love to go to Kerry, but they have never been nearer than Killarney.' These words of Samuel Murray Hussey (1824–1913), an infamous landlord's agent, distil better than anything the intent of this book – to move away from the well-beaten tourist paths and reveal the wider and deeper dimensions of Kerry.

I have to confess my handicap in this respect from the outset; I am one of the Killarney breed who drive our neighbours in Tralee, Dingle and Kenmare to distraction with notions that our lakeland valley is Heaven itself. But the remarkable thing is that it practically is. See how the malaise can take hold and take care, because neither visitor nor native is immune to the spell of our mountains and lakes.

On a more serious note, I have made it my business in my research to travel down narrow roads and into hinterlands where guesthouse signs and rental cars are as scarce as the proverbial hens' teeth. In the case of the main towns and well-known routes, I have gone beyond surface appearances to narrate personal histories and to introduce remarkable local characters that you will not find in brochures or guidebooks. The chronology is roughly from the 1500s through to the twentieth century, the eclectic pendulum of subject matter swinging with the verve of a Russian gymnast from the beheading of the Earl of Desmond in 1583 to a special birthday celebration for Big Bertha, the cow, in 1992.

Kerry is known as 'the Kingdom', but the county is far from a singular experience; there are kingdoms within kingdoms. The easiest distinction to make is based on the southern and northern divide: South Kerry, where generations survived on mountainy farms, pulled themselves up on the camera straps of dollared 'yanks', composed poems or took the boat or plane, and North Kerry of moneyed Tralee, the great fertile plain, the milch cow, the writers, the balladeers and the Norman castles and estates. Other little kingdoms include the legendary *Sliabh Luachra* floating to the east and famed for traditional music married to floor-pounding set dancing, the 'highlands' of Glencar and *Bealach Oisín* (Ballaghisheen) in the centre of the Ring of Kerry, and 'Over the Water' with its stone forts and deserted beaches, near Cahersiveen. In Dingle town you may think you have arrived in West Kerry until you overhear locals talking about heading 'back west', signifying Ballyferriter or Dunquin out on the peninsula. Incidentally, I probed a Dingle friend about possible hidden places to write about, only to get the following response (minus the expletives): 'I have a theory that tourists shouldn't be told about hidden places; we need a few that will still be our own to get away from them.'

This book's journey begins at Tarbert on the River Shannon, where many of the county's early settlers made their entrance, and finishes close to the Cork border under the ancient twin peaks of the Paps Mountains. Writing it has been as good, if not better, than a semester at university for me. I have refreshed my mind on half-forgotten dramas and discovered many new places and characters. It has given me an appreciation of an era in Kerry history when Europe was possibly a far more palpable reality for our forebears, through defensive alliances with the Catholic monarchies of France, Spain, Portugal and Italy, than it is for us today. The North Kerry boyhood of Lord Kitchener of the iconic war recruitment posters, Jesse James' ancestry in Asdee of the 'Moving Statues', the link between James Joyce's family and Lixnaw, and the electioneering antics of 'Tom Doodle' in Listowel all fascinated me, as I hope they will you.

Walking along Bromore Cliffs outside Ballybunion on a still and frosty November afternoon is one of the experiences that will remain with me. Another is listening to Ursula Leslie's stories as the evening drew in around Tarbert House, where scarcely a chair or a floor tile has been changed since the days when Benjamin Franklin, Charlotte Brontë and Daniel O'Connell crossed the threshold (obviously not all together). To sit in the porch of Tony Walsh's house on Valentia Island and to hear him relate stories such as a boat outing to the Great Blasket to dance sets in Peig Sayers' kitchen was pure gold.

When I meet visitors who have taken a guided tour of the Dingle Peninsula, I ask them, 'Did they tell you the one about the German commander whose U-boat surfaced in Ventry Harbour during the Second World War to put a party of Greek sailors ashore?' I knew about this humanitarian episode of old, but the escape plan hatched for Marie Antoinette in Dingle was a find for me, even though it is so often recounted 'back west' as to be unremarkable; you see a few mountain passes can make our little kingdoms insular.

Many Kerry people, myself included, had all but forgotten

that Margaret Thatcher was descended from a Kenmare washerwoman until the story resurfaced when she died. Among the characters who stand out for me are Albinia Brodrick, who turned her back on society life in London to build a hospital near Castlecove on the Ring of Kerry; Cornie Tangney of Scartaglin, who epitomised the spirit of individuality that once marked village life in Kerry; Mrs Elizabeth Herbert, who threw up her life in Muckross House to run away with her lover; and Fr Francis O'Sullivan, a gun-running friar who was beheaded on Scariff Island by Cromwellian soldiers. Some of the most moving stories I came across concern the terrible suffering of Kerry people during the famine years of the 1840s: lonely roads leading to the workhouses, the sundering of families, deaths from disease and hunger and mass graves.

Apart from Kerry's people and its landscapes, one of the county's great hidden treasures is its language: the Irish language as it is still spoken, mostly but not exclusively in the Gaeltacht areas, and the particular Kerry brand of Hiberno-English which draws heavily from the Irish. I have written principally about the latter. *Bhain mé ard shult as seo* (I got great enjoyment out of this) and I hope it will help to keep some of the words and expressions in currency.

I have always made it a priority to be a tourist in my own county but, being a creature of habit, I have tended to go back to my old haunts. This book is as much for the locals as it is for the visitors, to nudge ourselves beyond the familiar and to venture a little further into the paradise we are blessed to live in. What I am conscious of at the end of the day is that a wealth of other places, characters and happenings are still out there waiting to be chronicled. If your corner is not covered this time out, be patient with me, I could be back.

Slán go fóill

Arresting Experience

Tarbert (*Tairbeart*: 'peninsula') is a 'drive thru' town for most people: roll off or on the car ferry and continue down the road to Kerry or up the coast through Clare and Galway. But this was not always the case. The list of illustrious visitors to the Shannonside village reads like a 'Who's Who' of the literary and political world of earlier centuries: Benjamin Franklin, Charlotte Brontë, Daniel O'Connell, Horatio Herbert Kitchener, Winston Churchill and Dean Jonathan Swift. Their chief port of call was Tarbert House, dating from 1690 and still home to the Leslie family, who played a key role in the prosperity of the town in the heyday epoch of the 1800s. One of the many treasures from the house's past is a signed parchment application for Catholic Emancipation, which Daniel O'Connell made to the British House of Commons in 1813.

From 1 May to the end of August, Tarbert House, located at the end of a tree-lined drive opening off the road to the ferry, is open to the public. The custodian of the house and of the family history is Ursula Leslie. A native of Limerick, Ursula was a young barrister enjoying London life to the hilt in the mid-1960s when she met her future husband, John Leslie from Tarbert, on an Aer Lingus flight. To step across the threshold of Ursula's home and stand in the entrance hall is to enter a world little changed since all those famous visitors alighted on the banks of the Shannon to sample the Leslie hospitality.

Winston Churchill was related to the Leslies through an aunt who married into the family, and he spent some of his boyhood holidays there. Charlotte Brontë visited in 1854; she had just married her father's curate, Arthur Bell Nicholls, and they were on their way to Killarney on honeymoon. She suffered from tuberculosis and, in March 1855, died at the age of thirty-eight, along with her unborn child. Benjamin Franklin came to visit Sir Edward Leslie, then a Westminster MP, as part of a mission in 1776 to strengthen trade between Ireland and the American republic, then in its cradle days. Lord Kitchener was a young boy when his family lived for a time on an estate between Tarbert and Glin in County Limerick, and he revisited Tarbert House in 1910 as part of a holiday tour. Dean Swift wrote, 'The Leslies have lots of books upon their shelves. All written by Leslies about themselves.'

One of countless colourful anecdotes related by Ursula Leslie, a no-holds-barred conversationalist, is that of the visit of John Paul Jones, a commander in the US Continental Navy, on a 'terrible night' in 1778. Jones weighed anchor in Tarbert after two British gunboats pursued him; he had just sunk two British boats in Carlingford as part of the conflict that had ensued after the Declaration of Independence. At the time, the British marines leased Tarbert House, and Jones sent men ashore to create the illusion of sails with lanterns threaded through tree branches. With the aid of this ruse, he escaped down the Shannon, onto Valentia Island and back to America.

The hall at Tarbert House was tiled for a reason: cockfighting was a gentleman's sport in the 1800s. Ursula demonstrated how the backs of the hall chairs were designed to fit together as a circle. After dinner, the gentlemen sat astride the circle of chairs to watch the unfortunate birds fight to the death with spurs and claws.

The Leslie coat of arms features a thistle, three buckles and the motto 'Grip Fast'. Its origins are attributed to a Hungarian nobleman, Bartholomew, the first Leslie to arrive in Scotland in 1067. He is said to have been protecting Queen Margaret, the wife of King Malcolm III of Scotland, when she was swept from her horse into a river after a buckle broke. As he rescued her from the torrent, Bartholomew said, 'Grip fast, my lady.'

Decorative carvings featuring the Shannon's bottle-nosed dolphins embellish the hall couch. Other motifs include wheat sheaves, a rope and boats. Other interesting features of the hallway are the musket and bayonet racks and the trestles dating back to the time of the first Kerry Volunteers, formed to guard against a feared offensive by Napoleon's forces on the Shannon in the late 1700s.

The dining room has all the original furniture, including two gilded Chippendale mirrors carved from one piece of wood. The Leslies were connected through marriage to the Chutes of Tralee, and a silver trophy in the dining room belonged to Trevor Chute.

An entirely different window on Kerry life opens a little further down the road from Tarbert House, at the Tarbert Bridewell Courthouse & Jail Museum, where the exhibition reveals the harsh life of the poverty-stricken classes who were imprisoned or transported to penal colonies during the 1830s. The Tarbert Bridewell was one of eight new bridewells constructed in Kerry between 1828 and 1829. Among the bizarre sentences listed in the exhibition is seven years' transportation for stealing a book entitled *A Summary Account on the Flourishing State of the Island of Tobago*. Jonathan Binns, writing in 1837, suggested that there were cases in North Kerry where men 'had committed petty thefts for the sole purpose of being transported'. Another detail recorded is that the Knight of Glin, who spent his time helping the poor during the Great Famine, died in 1854 from cholera he contracted while visiting a workhouse.

In 1887 John Redmond, who was subsequently to become leader of the Irish Parliamentary Party, defended nine local men who were tried at Tarbert Bridewell for holding an illegal Land League meeting. One of the few Land League flags still extant in Ireland is on display here. It was recovered from the thatch of the Lavery homestead in Church Street in the 1950s and emblazoned with the words 'Tarbert National League'. It was embroidered by Mrs Lavery, whose husband was treasurer of the group.

The bridewell is the starting point for my walking tour with Patrick J. Lynch, the author of *Tarbert: An Unfinished Biography* and chairman of the Tarbert Historical and Heritage Society. Patrick explains that Tarbert primarily developed as a harbour town and that, in the early years, it was a busy port for ships delivering goods for the south-west of Ireland. It was well known as a natural harbour and was often used by boats to shelter from storms. During the night of the Big Wind in 1839, a total of thirty-seven schooners took shelter in Tarbert.

Patrick presents an eyewitness account of Famine-time Tarbert thanks to a batch of letters written by Dr Thomas Graham, who was stationed on the HMS *Madagascar*. The British relief ship was based in Tarbert from 1846 to 1848 as a grain carrier for the south-west of Ireland. Patrick describes the importance of the letters the doctor wrote to his sister at home in Scotland, the lucid style and humanitarian nature of which shed great light on the area at the time. The doctor gives a graphic account of helping people during the Famine years. While he was only supposed to look after the people on the *Madagascar*, it seems he was unable to refuse locals who urged him to help their sick. He writes of going into cabins and having to wipe away the tears from the smoke as he tried to alleviate the suffering. The letters are simply an invaluable insight into Tarbert of the time.

Patrick explains that travel in the 1800s was often by water, making Tarbert a place of strategic importance in the south-west of Ireland. People travelling south from Dublin went by road or canal to Limerick and transferred to Tarbert, where they continued their journey by sea or by Bianconi coach. (The strategic location of the town came into its own once again in 1969 when the Shannon ferry service between Tarbert and Killimer was inaugurated, linking Kerry and Clare. It is a daily, year-round service.)

The insatiable demand for food and agricultural produce created by the Napoleonic Wars in the 1800s rippled all the way up the Shannon to Tarbert and boosted the harbour town's trade hugely. As a result of this wave of trade and prosperity, Tarbert acquired a lighthouse, built on a tidal rock to the north of Tarbert Island in 1831; its population had grown to 1,046 by 1846. But, as Patrick points out, the boom was to be followed by a bust, in the normal cycle of economies. 'The advent of the rail link to Foynes in Limerick in 1858 sounded the death knell for Tarbert,' he says.

Staying with the boom for now, the ferry road running past the bridewell leads to Tarbert's piers, built in 1837 and 1859 to service the thriving export trade in corn, butter and pigs. On their return journeys, the ships were loaded with coal, iron and steel. In that era, Tarbert boasted two towering general providers' stores: Pattersons (1839), which stood where Tarbert's e-Town is located, across the road from the bridewell, and the six-storey Russells' Store (1847) on its town side.

Patrick points out the surviving stone perimeter wall of Russells' Store. Set into the wall is a series of twelve beautifully wrought bronze plaques telling the story of Tarbert and its hinterland from St Senan in the early Christian period right up to the development of the electricity generating station on Tarbert Island in the 1960s. This work of art is reason alone to stop the car in Tarbert. The bronzes, entitled *A Storied Shannonside*, are the work of artists Liam Lavery and Eithne Ring. Across the street the orange façade of the Swanky Bar provides a striking contrast.

The Green river runs beside Russells' wall. The walking tour Patrick gives me follows the riverside path beside it and across the footbridge which leads around to Memorial Plaza where two plaques commemorate the district's war dead and the Tarbert boating tragedy of 1893. This Shannon tragedy claimed the lives of seventeen people, including seven women, who had been returning from an excursion to County Clare on 15 August, a holy day and a festival day throughout Kerry. It is believed that the boat, one of two that travelled that day, was overcrowded and unseaworthy. The loss of life left a deep mark on the psyche of the community.

Of the eleven Tarbert men who died in the First World War, six of them were under the age of twenty-five. Among them was Michael Lynch, who died in northern France on the Belgian border in 1916, at the age of twenty. He was Patrick Lynch's uncle. From the Memorial Plaza, we walk back up into the town, passing Coolahan's Bar, in business since 1887, the site of the Munster Bank (1872) and the former AIB Bank, whose closure in 2012 symbolises the demise in Tarbert's fortunes.

Patrick points out the corner building, the Ferry Hostel, and says it stands on the site of the former Leslie Arms Hotel, which was one arm of the planned estate town developed by Sir Edward Leslie. We continue down Church Street, which becomes the Limerick Road; Glin in County Limerick, seat of the Knights of Glin, is only four miles away. Patrick points out the most significant building on this street: the two-storey house to the left which was the home of Tarbert's most illustrious son of contemporary times, Thomas MacGreevy (1893–1967). Twice wounded at the Somme, MacGreevy was a poet, a literary and art critic, and director of the National Gallery in Dublin from 1950 to 1963. He moved to Paris in 1927 and became a personal friend of James Joyce and Samuel Beckett. Academic Susan Schreibman, in an article in *The Kerry Magazine*, wrote that his poetry captured an Ireland 'unsure of the way forward and uneasy about its past'. She said that his genius was that he was not simply attuned to what was happening in Ireland, but to Europe as a whole. His most anthologised poem is 'Aodh Rua Ó Domhnaill'.

The day I visited Tarbert, the only sign of vibrancy was Tarbert Comprehensive School, where lines of cars and buses were waiting for the outpouring of students at 4 p.m. Yet something welling from the realms of hope tells me that the Shannon estuary will come into its own again through harnessing natural gas reserves, and the rising tide will lift Tarbert once more. In the meantime, do resist the temptation to drive through: switch off the ignition and savour the history of this storied Shannonside town.

Kitchener's Kerry

O ne of the most iconic images of the twentieth century, that of a mustachioed military figure staring out from the First World War recruitment posters, is that of a Kerryman.
Or is it?
Field Marshal Horatio Herbert Kitchener was born at Gunsborough Villa, three miles from Listowel, on 24 June 1850. This undoubtedly makes him a Kerryman by birth, but whether the distinguished British Army officer regarded himself as such is a matter of debate. According to Listowel author Fr Anthony Gaughan, Kitchener was not particularly proud of his Irish origins or nationality. Reminded of his birth in Ireland, the field marshal is reported to have quoted the Duke of Wellington: 'A man can be born in a stable and not be a horse.'
However, the fact that the famous military figure took the

trouble to revisit the North Kerry of his boyhood as an adult suggests that he placed some importance on the fact that he was a Kerryman and an Irishman by birth. In June 1910 Kitchener visited his Kerry childhood haunts: Gunsborough, Crotta, Listowel, Tarbert, Ballygoghlan, Ballybunion and Tralee. A news report in *The Kerryman* of Saturday 25 June 1910 gave the following account of his visit to Killarney, where he stayed in the Victoria Hotel:

> Lord Kitchener enjoyed his trip through the Lower, Middle and Upper Lakes yesterday immensely. He stated that it had been forty years since he had been in Killarney last, and he sincerely hoped he would be able to visit it oftener in the future. He was charmed with the scenery and the weather was ideal.

The report went on to relate how he had signed the hotel's 'distinguished roll' and posed for photographs with the proprietor before leaving for Derreen, the residence of the marquess of Lansdowne, en route to Cork via Glengariff. 'His lordship charmed everybody with whom he came in contact in the Lake and district by his extreme graciousness and affability and carried away with him the God-speed of everybody,' it concluded. In July 1910 Kitchener wrote from Roche's Hotel (now the Parknasilla Hotel) near Sneem to the Leslies of Tarbert House suggesting that he and his brother would call for lunch.

Retired garda superintendent and local historian Donal J. O'Sullivan, a Corkman, posited in an article for the Kerry Archaeological & Historical Society that Kitchener was the best-known Kerryman internationally. He has subsequently admitted that this claim did not meet with a great reception in some corners of Kerry. In fact, I would hazard that Kitchener's Kerry connection is one of the county's best-kept secrets.

Kitchener's birthplace is a story in itself. Gunsborough Villa, which still stands near the village of Ballylongford, was located twelve miles from Ballygoghlan, between Tarbert and Glin, where the future field marshal's father, Colonel Henry Horatio Kitchener, had bought a bankrupt estate around 1850. Kitchener Senior had served with the British Army in India, and his introduction to North Kerry may have come through his brother, Philip, who was a land agent for the Earl of Dunraven in Adare, County Limerick. Possibly because the estate house was still being refurbished, the heavily pregnant Fanny Kitchener was staying at Gunsborough, which, according to Donal O'Sullivan, belonged to a family friend and retired clergyman, Robert Sandes. The fact that Kitchener was baptised by Revd Robert Wren Sandes in Aghavallen Church of Ireland near Ballylongford the following September suggests that the stay was a prolonged one.

The health of Fanny Kitchener, a vicar's daughter, was precarious; she suffered from acute deafness and had contracted tuberculosis. Gaughan relates that Henry Kitchener was forced to leave his regiment in India and return to England in 1847 because of his wife's ill-health. She gave birth to two more sons while the family was still living in Kerry: Arthur Buck in 1852 and Walter in 1858.

Her husband's reinvention as a landlord on the estate close to the Shannon estuary appeared to bring him a measure of prosperity. According to Gaughan, Kitchener Senior was a harsh landlord who was resented because he had a notorious habit of whipping his tenants. The tables were allegedly turned on him on one occasion when the Knight of Glin, John Fraunceis Eyre Fitzgerald, whipped Colonel Kitchener at the Tralee Races. It is not certain that the Knight's action was motivated by the treatment of the tenants.

The family lived mostly at a second property, Crotta Great House, near the village of Kilflynn. The Kitcheners purchased Crotta, which has a fascinating history of its own, around 1852. It was here that Horatio spent most of his North Kerry boyhood; he was about fourteen years of age when the family severed their ties with the county of his birth. The family worshipped in the Church of Ireland church in the village of Kilflynn. The 'Kitchener Memorial Bible', first presented to the church after Kitchener's death, has since been entrusted to Saint John's Church of Ireland in Ashe Street, Tralee.

And what of the boy Kitchener? Gaughan recounts an incident, recorded by Mrs C. E. Gourley in her book *They Walked beside the River Shannow*, in which he struck one of his father's staff, Jamsey Sullivan, with his riding crop as Sullivan was felling trees in a wood. Sullivan retaliated by hitting out at Kitchener, who fell from his horse and was knocked unconscious. The incident is described in this way:

> Fear gripped the other workmen. It was during the agrarian troubles and had the boy Kitchener died they would have been accused of murdering the landlord's son. The lad recovered and won the respect of the men for his sense of justice – he did not tell his father, nor have Jamsey punished.

The young Kitcheners were educated at home by tutors, a regime that was said to have left them lagging behind their peers academically. In 1864 the family moved from Kerry to Switzerland in the vain hope that the climate there would improve Fanny's health, but she died during the summer of that year, at the age of thirty-nine. Kitchener was deeply saddened at the loss of his mother. At boarding school in Switzerland, Kitchener keenly felt the disadvantage of his home schooling. It has been suggested that this experience of feeling inferior spurred him to be a tireless achiever. In 1867 his father remarried and moved to Dunedin on New Zealand's South Island. Kitchener and his brother Walter spent the school holidays with relatives in Britain because their father had left them behind when he emigrated. This, coupled with his beloved mother's early death, must have had a huge psychological impact on Kitchener.

His military career saw him serve on numerous overseas postings and won him the admiration of the British parliament, which rewarded him with the title 'Baron of Khartoum'. His subsequent campaign in the Boer War was marked by unprecedented savagery. He went on to become Secretary of State for War in 1914. The famous recruitment posters, which enjoy an enduring currency no one could have predicted, have made his face instantly recognisable right into the twenty-first century.

Kitchener was killed near the Orkney Islands off Scotland on 5 June 1916 when the warship on which he was travelling to Russia was sunk by a German mine; his body was never recovered. Horatio Herbert Kitchener went a long way for a boy who might have lost his life in a fall from a horse in a Kerry wood.

Fealeside

W here the River Feale loops like a sickle between the Listowel racecourse and the town, the sound of the racing water rises up into Tea Lane and the *Gleann*. If you are a local, tea is pronounced tae, and the *Gleann*'s full title is *Gleannaphouca* or the Glen of the Fairies. The *Gleann* stretches for about a quarter of a mile along the river line, taking in, above it, a street of little houses where coopers and other craftsmen plied their trade.

The Feale was a natural playground for youngsters like Michael Guerin growing up in the houses of the *Gleann* in the 1950s. From Lent, when the boys began to fish for brown trout, into June and July, when the white sea trout came up the river in shoals, the river was the centre of their lives. Upstream on the Island Bridge, visible from the terrace of the Listowel Arms Hotel, they dived into a deep pool. The Mill Dam, downstream at Greenville, was another natural meeting place. Sawdust pitched from the bars high up in Market Street down the Market Cliff to the riverbank at the end of fair days was often a source of treasure when the river washed coins out of it. Schoolmaster and writer Bryan MacMahon captured the emotional currency of the river in a song, 'My Silver River Feale'.

Such were the lyrical topics that occupied Michael Guerin and myself when we surveyed the river from the terrace of the Listowel Arms, a venue that has hosted some of the top names in literature since the Listowel Writers' Week was founded in 1970. Michael shared with me a poem written by the late Seán Ashe about the houses of the *Gleann*, which once formed the most populated street in Listowel. Seán was a reporter for local and national papers as well as running a shop with his sister, Nora. His talent as a wordsmith is evident in the following verse from his poem:

> Now homeward come the brawny men,
> At close of hard-worked day.
> The caged birds sing their vesper song,
> Back all along the way.
> The Convent Bell its age-old spell,
> I hear it ringing down.
> Its hopeful message to retell,
> 'Tis evening in the *Gleann*.

Listowel translates as *Lios Tuathail*, or Tuathail's Fort, and in the fine town square I prompted my guide for stories of the occupants of the houses there – I had some memory of Bryan MacMahon talking about piano music cascading through an open window in the evenings. Michael responded with an anecdote about a notorious landlord's agent, George Sandes, who was said to have 'died the gander's death' in one of the houses. This was a new expression to my innocent Killarney ears. How do I explain it … in delicate terms? The gander's death besets a person in the throes of passion or *in flagrante delicto*. Stories of the rapacious Mr Sandes were still very alive in the minds of Michael's uncles when he was growing up. The agent was said to prey without shame on the daughters of tenants, declaring, 'If you haven't the rent book, send me your daughters.'

Leaving all thoughts of priapic ganders behind us, we walked towards Listowel Castle, built by the Fitzmaurices in the fifteenth century, and noted the image of a face about halfway up the right side of the façade. To the rear of the castle once stood a sweet factory, North Kerry Manufacturing. Here, the river walk would bring us all the way out to the Big Bridge on the Tralee Road but we opted to continue through the Square, passing The Seanchaí (Kerry Writers' Museum) and Saint Mary's church. The corner house on our right as we left the square was eye-catching for the standard of the decorative plasterwork. On our left as we walked down Bridge Road was Gurtenard House, dating back to the 1830s. Now privately owned, it has been home to a number of families, including the Collis', Fitzgeralds and Armstrongs. The Earl and Countess of Listowel entertained the local gentry there between 1870 and 1890.

Turning left into the town park, Childers Park, our conversation switched to the writer and balladeer, Seán McCarthy (1923–90), a Listowel man who spent his final days in the North Kerry village of Finuge and whose best-known ballad is 'Shanagolden'. Michael related how Seán used to joke that the family had a swimming pool front and back when they were growing up on the Forge Road – bog holes. But we recalled too a darker story, which inspired Seán's song, 'In Shame Love, In Shame', which had its roots in a far less tolerant Ireland. One of Seán's sisters was single when she became pregnant and because of this she was refused admittance to the hospitals in Listowel and Tralee while in labour. Her cruel journey ended in the County Home in Killarney where she died giving birth to a baby girl. When her funeral cortège arrived back in Listowel, the gates of St Mary's church were locked and chained. It took the intervention of some locals to have the coffin admitted. Seán McCarthy was extremely hurt at the callous treatment of his sister and wrote the song in her memory.

While we remembered Seán and his sister, we sat near the Dandy Lodge at the entrance to the park. The gate lodge, originally located outside Lord Listowel's house on Bridge Road, was transferred across the road brick by brick in 1997. From here we continued through the park to the banks of the Feale beside the Big Bridge and followed the river to the Garden of Europe, a fresh discovery for me though I visit Listowel often. The sculpture garden is a must-see and was developed on a site which was, in earlier existences, the town dump and a quarry that supplied the stone for the construction of much of Listowel. Our walk continued through the graveyard on Church Road and back into the town centre from where we did another loop, taking in the Lartigue Monorail museum and the Famine graveyard, *Teampaillín Bán*. North Kerry's railways, including the Lartigue, are one of the passions of Michael, who wrote and published *The Lartigue Monorailways* in 1988 and assisted in the publication of *The North Kerry Line* by Dr Alan O'Rourke in 2013. Proceeds of this book will go towards the Great Southern Trail from Limerick to Tralee. The original steam-powered monorail, designed by Frenchman Charles Lartigue, ran for nine miles between Listowel and the seaside resort of Ballybunion between 1888 and 1924. The museum, located in a former goods shed, is a short distance from Listowel, just off the Ballybunion Road.

The Street

❦

C hurch Street in Listowel, a street of scholars and craftsmen, has been immortalised in verse by John B. Keane, who spent his boyhood there before decamping a roofline away to William Street, where the family bar is located. His poem 'The Street' features in an illustrated wall display opposite Listowel Garda Station.

Among the learned characters who came from Church Street was Mai Quillinan, a former librarian who retired to No. 15 where her aunts had run a confectioner's. Mai was aged eighty-five when I met her in the course of my work as a journalist writing about streets across Kerry in 1991. Having discovered that we shared the same birthday, we sipped sherry from Waterford Crystal to toast our good health. A Listowel woman, Mai had worked at Kilmainham Library in Dublin and had amassed priceless memories during her time in the capital, among them recollections of meeting the Anglo-Irish patriot Countess Markievicz in the home of Tralee republican Austin Stack and his wife Winnie in Dublin's Strand Street. The highlight of Sunday afternoons in the Stack home was the arrival of the Countess, who was known as 'Madame' in that social circle. Mai recalled how the Countess would take out a beautiful gold cigarette case and offer it around, but the strange thing was that there were only Woodbines inside. According to Mai, she could not afford more expensive cigarettes as she had given most of her money away to the poor. The Listowel woman described the aristocrat in this way: 'She was as thin as a whip and not very well. She would go in by the fire and sit on a little stool with a cushion on top. She was a chain smoker and hardly ate at all.'

Across Church Street, at No. 38, lived Mai's close friends, the writer Bryan MacMahon and his wife Kitty. Even though Kitty had lived on Church Street for fifty-four years at that stage, she was still very attached to the memory of her childhood garden, which ran right up to the Rock of Cashel in Tipperary and had apple trees entwined with mistletoe. When her sons went for walks in springtime Listowel as boys, they brought her pocketfuls of primroses. MacMahon, a gracious man of patrician bearing, introduced the workshop concept to Writers' Week with John B. As well as being a gifted short-story writer, he was an imaginative teacher. Once, when a circus came to town, he 'borrowed' a young elephant and brought it into the school to illustrate a lesson.

Down the street from the MacMahons, at No. 30, was Flavin's Bookshop, where Dan Flavin slaked the literary thirst of Listowel with volume after volume of the classics. I have a memory of MacMahon telling me that when he bought his copy of *Ulysses* there, the pages were still uncut.

Church Street married the world of scholars and learning to the world of craftsmen and trade. Former National University of Ireland Registrar Seamus Wilmot, MacMahon, John B. Keane and his actor brother, Eamonn, whose voice was described as a 'fusion of *poitín* and honey', and Joseph O'Connor, author of a wonderful memoir, *Hostage to Fortune*, all lived there.

O'Connor's reminiscences of the street include his grandfather, 'Old Joe' Wilmot, who came from 'an unbroken line of smiths whose beginnings were traced to a Joe Wilmot, farrier to a troop of Cromwellian cavalry'. Other Church Street craftsmen of that bygone age, now preserved between the pages of his book, include 'Jackie the Nailer', who made hobnails for 'Patsy the Cobbler'. He laments the passing of Jackie and the rest of the street's artisan class as follows: 'Gone, too, are Matt Quill and Corridan, the cooper, and Eddie Wilmot, the last blacksmith of his name. With them went the neighbourly din of their looms and teames and anvils and the lore of past generations'.

The decorative plasterwork of Pat McAuliffe, described by MacMahon as 'the God of Listowel', is still resplendent in Church Street and all over Listowel, making it a town where it is advised to keep looking up to the first and second storeys of buildings. The two examples of his artistry in Church Street are the Harp and Lion Bar and, high up on Mai Quillinan's former home at No. 15, the Phoenix Pluribus, which reveals the street's old name, *Sráid an Ághasaigh*, or Ashe Street.

The song of the anvil has long since melted into a silence that has also enveloped the harnessmakers, shoemakers, weavers, coopers and bakers of Church Street, but they have left a legacy of vibrancy in their wake.

Thomas Xavier Doodle

A s election manifestos go, it was certainly inventive: to erect a factory for shaving the hair off gooseberries, to ensure a vote for *lorgadauns* and leprechauns, and to plough the Rocks of Bawn (this last pledge was a reference to a patriotic ballad). The maverick candidate, who burst on the scene during the Irish general election campaign of 1951, owed his existence and that of his followers, the Independent Coulogeous Party, to the fertile imagination of playwright John B. Keane, who explained, 'We invented a character in Listowel called Thomas Xavier Doodle, TD, and we invented him to take the bitterness out of politics.' The bitterness he was referring to was the backwash of the Irish Civil War, which, though at a remove of thirty years, still had the power to incite powerful passions fuelled largely by atrocities committed on both sides of the divide.

Fergal Keane, journalist and nephew of John B., wrote that, like every Irish election campaign since the partition of the country, this one too had been dominated by Civil War politics: 'The stuff which was kept under wraps most of the time came flooding out in elections: who had fought on what side, who had killed who, who had really represented the will of the Irish people.' According to Keane, both sides 'were limbering up for an orgy of bile and insults … into this hotbed of simmering tensions stepped the highly original Tom Doodle, as he was affectionately known, who took the north Kerry public by storm at a Monster Rally attended by an estimated 3,000 people in the Small Square in Listowel in June 1951.'

The putative politician, a friend of John B., arrived by train, having boarded at Kilmorna just a short distance up the line, and was preceded to his speaking engagement by two town bands. His unifying powers were evident from the outset as John B. pointed out: 'The two bands fused for the first time in years – they hadn't been getting on.' The author also had the boast that a meeting of the Taoiseach John A. Costello had only attracted 1,000 people the previous night. 'Vote the Noodle and give the whole Kaboodle to Doodle' the crowd was exhorted at the close of the rally, which was followed by the Grand Dinner of the Independent Coulogeous Party in the Listowel Arms Hotel. The dinner menu read, 'Mackerels' Cods, *Pinkeens* (small fish), Sprat, Pate de FreeGaol, Birds' Eggs, Bees' Knees and Lettuce, Humps of Camel, Ostrich Buttock and Linnet Sauce'. The programme included a lecture, 'How to Survive on Goodwill' and 'Drink, Song and Merriment until Porter is Exhausted'. The proceedings drew to a close with a rendition of the 'Doodle Anthem'.

An entire mythology has since grown up around that brief interlude of adult make-believe; they say that the name Tom Doodle even appeared on some of the ballot sheets. Through the madcap humour of his creation, John B. poked fun at po-faced electioneering and went a long way to closing the chasm of residual bitterness dividing people. It was just one example of the deep humanity and compassion that characterised the writer, who assessed the episode as follows: 'It was nonsense but it knocked the bitterness out of politics. Bitterness is an awful weight to carry. It creates nothing. The frost of it is still there.'

The Smearlagh Way

W hen bodhrán-maker Thady Gunn of Listowel was fashioning one of the traditional Irish instruments, a cross between a drum and a tambourine, he would roll a goatskin in lime and immerse it in the Smearlagh river to draw the music of the river into it. Fr Pat Moore, a North Kerry priest and my guide, related this anecdote as we passed Thady Gunn's house at the start of our journey through the Smearlagh Valley. The road traverses the heartland of Listowel, and just as the river is a water source for North Kerry, the valley and its characters proved a source of inspiration for John B. Keane's writing, including his novel *The Bodhrán Makers*, which is set in the 1950s.

At the centre of this patchwork of bog and high fields rolling across the Stack's Mountains is the parish of Lyreacrompane. *Ladhar an Chrompáin* translates as the fork in the river valley (locals use the abbreviated form, 'Lyre'). It was the birthplace of the last of the great Irish matchmakers, Dan Paddy Andy O'Sullivan (1899–1966), who was immortalised in John B.'s play *The Matchmaker*. You can approach Lyre from Abbeyfeale or Castleisland but, today, to follow the course of the Smearlagh river, we turn right off the bridge on the Tralee side of Listowel town and onto the R555 or Abbeyfeale Road. After about a mile, we turn right into a road scarcely the width of the car and shortly pass the former home of the bodhrán-maker on our left.

The river's Irish name, *An Smeárlach*, is possibly linked to the blackberries (*smeára dubha*) which are ripening in tangles of briars all along the banks of the tumbling river this August. On either side of the gradually rising road are green fields marked with clumps of rushes and, in places, purple loosestrife. The sound of the Smearlagh flowing over rocks below us rises up to the high road; wind turbines loom on the horizon beyond the townland of Athea and blankets of forestry are spread on the landscape ahead of us.

In the townland of Knockaunbrack Lower, located eight miles from both Listowel and Abbeyfeale, lives Michael Fahy, a Galway man and yoga teacher, with his wife, Amanda, and their two daughters. The holding, once the home of Maryanne Doody and her husband, Mossie, was connected to the since demolished Knockalougha National School by a footbridge. While the life and the light went out of many homes in the area when the old people passed, the Fahys have brought new life with them, as Michael relates. 'When I came here, people couldn't understand how I could retreat out here. Normally, people leave here. That was a big mystery to people.'

Round his table, set out with scones and spelt bread, homemade blackberry jam and home-grown greens and tomatoes, the conversation turns to the Famine story of the 'hungry grass'. Pat says his mother told him that cattle and horses would get weak in a certain part of the field where poor people had died of hunger. 'It was grass where people of the Famine lay down and died and weren't buried,' he said. There's talk of energies in places and landscapes, and Michael Fahy believes that the good intentions, the energy and the sacredness of Maryanne Doody (who lived in the house before him) lived on there after she passed. Both Pat and Michael were friends of the philosopher and writer, John Moriarty, who came from outside Listowel. 'I spent two weeks going around Kerry with John Moriarty looking for radiance in the landscape when he was looking for a site to build a house,' Pat smiles. 'John used to say that there are certain people who allow the countryside to speak through them, and Mike Fahy is one of these.' In the house where John Moriarty was to end his days, in sight of the Horse's Glen in Muckross, he used to drop wisps of his grey hair, loosened by chemotherapy, out the bathroom window. A finch gathered them and wove them into the curve of its nest. When the young were flown and the nest abandoned, John brought it inside the house to join his collection of 'totems'.

Stories like this could have lasted the livelong day around the Fahys' table, but we continue up the road to Enright's Bridge, where the end of the white fingerpost sign pointing for Lyreacrompane looks as if it's been bitten off. The Smearlagh turns with us, racing along at the base of an ancient and flourishing oak wood.

John B. Keane wrote of Lyreacrompane and its hinterland:

I fell immediately in love with this strange and wonderful countryside, with the character, colour and language of the people, and its numerous dancing streams. The unbound freedom of hills and glens amounted to sheer paradise. The Stack's have magic all of their own where the green meadows merge into boglands. The dominating colour is brown but, ever and always, it is a brown that is warm and comforting.

Lyreacrompane, Pat explains, enjoyed a prosperity based on its bogland and the turf it yielded. The first tractor in the area was bought here, and a German expert, Harry Starken, was invited to set up turf-cutting machinery. One of his daughters, Elizabeth, who went on to become head of the Presentation Order in Ireland, gave the following insight into their Lyre lives:

> My father worked the bog, morning, noon and night. I can still hear the tap on the bedroom window when someone had to come and wake my father ... 'Harry, the bagger is stuck.' And my father would get out of bed in the middle of the night to fix the machine. Often, it was a piece of bogdeal. My roots are in Lyre, like that bog oak. In spite of the hard work, he loved that place as did we all.

During the 1940s Bord na Móna, the state body managing turf-cutting, was a dominant influence in the life of Lyreacrompane. Hundreds of workers were brought in by lorry from areas including Abbeyfeale, Tournafulla and Castlemaine to harvest the turf, which was used to power such industries as the sugar factory in Mallow, County Cork.

Behind the Sacred Heart church, a footbridge leads to the beginning of the Mass Path, or the Smearlagh Way, which follows the river down to the Lyreacrompane Community

Centre. The walk is dedicated to the memory of priest, poet and author, John O'Donohue (1956–2008), who is probably best known for his book, *Anam Cara*. The writer, a friend of Pat's, had planned the Munster launch of his book *Benedictus* at the centre in 2008, but it did not go ahead because of the author's death that year.

I will leave the final words on the river to Castleisland bard and wordsmith Con Houlihan, who once taught in Renagown National School 'in the heart of the great moorland that lies between Listowel and Castle Island'. He travelled the seven miles from his home to the schoolhouse by bike daily, and the journey inspired him to write these poetic lines, 'The last three miles are downhill; I flowed along by the infant Smearla; the fusion of spokesong and streamsong made lovely music.'

Bromore Cliffs

Lumps of sea-polished coal occasionally found among the stones below the waterfall at Bromore Cliffs near Ballybunion were originally destined for a far distant shore. The black diamonds were part of a cargo of 1,000 tons of gas coal dispatched from Glasgow on 11 November 1882 and intended to power gas lamps illuminating the streets and buildings of New York. But neither the coal nor its carrier, the *Dronningen*, which originated in Christiana, now known as Oslo, ever reached the city's docks. Relics of the sail ship, whose name means 'queen' in Norwegian, still persist around Ballybunion as reminders of the storm-tossed voyage that ended at Bromore: a flake of the anchor visible at low tide, a kitchen table and rafters fashioned from decking and timbers, all to the good after more than 130 years.

Horses once ploughed fields and pulled traps to Doon Chapel shod in shoes forged from the anchor chain links at Leahy's Forge at Bromore, which is located a mile outside Ballybunion on the road to Asdee. Mike Flahive's family has farmed the windswept green fields on the edge of Bromore Cliffs for generations; his great-grandfather was born there in 1829. When Mike wrote about the shipwreck in *The Shannonside Journal* in 1993, he had a personal link to the story: his grandfather was one of the locals who went to the aid of Captain Carl Anderson and his crew of sixteen after the ship ran aground near the Flahive farmhouse. The fury of a severe hurricane had overtaken the *Dronningen* about 500 miles off Achill Island and had blown it off course. Driven by winds of up to 100 knots and pounded by mountainous seas, the ship was unmanageable; the coal shifted with every lurch, threatening to destroy it from inside. On Monday 20 November 1882, at 6 p.m., the ship drifted within sight of Loop Head lighthouse across the Shannon from Bromore; it avoided the Clare cliffs by less than half a mile, but gigantic swells propelled the stricken vessel across to the Kerry coast and onto the shore at Poultenaw under Bromore Cliffs.

The captain and crew stayed on board until they were

rescued in the morning by local farmers alerted by a Mr Hunt from Doon, who spotted the tall masts rising over the cliffs. Captain Anderson was last to leave his ship and brought with him a beautiful young Newfoundland dog and a little pup in his pocket. The crew was taken to nearby farmhouses for dry clothes, food and rest, and returned on Thursday and Friday at low spring tide to salvage what little belongings were left.

Mike Flahive's grandfather, Dan Flahive, then seventeen, remembered the captain as 'a fine blond-haired man, over six feet tall with a beard'. The captain regaled the farmers with the tale of his last voyage and of others to New York and Quebec and to Murmansk around the North Cape, the land of the midnight sun. On Monday 4 December 1882 Robert McCown, as agent for Lloyd's, auctioned off the cargo of coal and ropes, rigging, blocks, spars and masts.

The fate of the Norwegian ship is just one episode in the storied past of Bromore Cliffs, which opened to the public in July 2012 when Mike Flahive and his wife, Eilish, developed an amenity walk on their farm. Another casualty of the cliffs dates back to the 1750s, when a French schooner sailing for Limerick and laden with fine wines ran aground at Carrigarone (the Seal's Rock).

Bromore, which takes its name from *brú mór*, big bank, is steeped in history: banks of shale 350 million years old and a geologist's paradise, the remnants of a defensive fort dating back over 1,500 years and a concrete lookout point from the Second World War. History aside, there are stunning clifftop views westwards to the blue mountain line of West Kerry and across the Shannon estuary to Loop Head in County Clare, which is literally a shout away. As Mike remarks, 'We used to hear them putting in the cows over in Clare on a calm evening.'

When I visited, late on a still, frosty November afternoon, the sea was an ethereal blue and a fading sun was spilling a pale yellow brilliance on the water. In Bromore you can watch a 'wet sun' setting in the sea between Kerry Head and Loop Head in County Clare from September through to March. From then on the sun stays 'dry' as it sinks behind the land of Loop Head. The 86-degree spread of the sunset winter to summer was always a measure of time for the Flahives, as Mike explains: 'The sunset was our clock here in Dromore – time to set the spuds, save the hay, time for Santa.'

Bromore is honeycombed with caves, some of them running about a mile under the Flahive farm. The Mermaids' Caves have five openings. Birds flock through the big-mouthed Starlings' Cave in late summer. Mike is more familiar than most with the caves that dot the coastline around Ballybunion because he is former Chief Coxswain of Ballybunion Sea and Cliff Rescue.

Another spectacular natural feature at Bromore is Glenachoor Waterfall, a narrow stream of water tumbling vertically from a height of 93 feet. Mike saw it frozen solid with a big pan of ice at its base in 1963. A stone column, known as The Stack or Devil's Castle, rising 120 feet out of the water, is often a perch for peregrines. Mike has an 1834 drawing of a smaller column, the Devil's Chair, showing it as an arch which has since collapsed.

At the eastern end of the walk is *Leamnamuice* (The Pigs' Jump) where, it is told, a brace of wild boar escaped from the legendary Irish leader, Fionn MacCumhaill, his soldiers, the Fianna, and their hounds by leaping across a chasm to safety.

The Bromore foxes, 'often hunted, never captured', are intrepid residents of a den opening onto an inaccessible ledge on the upper reaches of the cliffs.

Searching for Jesse James' Grandfather

Halfway between Ballybunion and Listowel, the people of the little village of Lisselton were out on the roadside hoping to catch a presidential wave as the cavalcade rolled through. But they were in for a surprise. Bill Clinton, arguably the most powerful politician in the world, made an unscheduled stop in Lisselton on 4 September 1998, on his way to the freshly painted seaside resort of 'Bally B' (as it is known in local parlance) for a round of golf on the famous links course. He got out of his car and shook hands with locals bedazzled by the white American smile.

Lisselton's gain that day was Listowel's loss. John B. Keane's bar, vetted and selected as an official stop, was packed to the rafters. But word had leaked out and a group of peaceful protestors gathered on the street outside. Once the 'Free Tibet' banner was unfurled, there was no question of the President of America sampling a pint at John B.'s; the cars booted out the Ballybunion Road to avoid controversy.

The September visit to Lisselton went into the village's history books, where another highly significant but little known American connection preceded it. As Clinton entered Lisselton, one of the houses he passed on the left-hand side of the road had a large key set above the door. This house was home to the writer Maurice Walsh (1879–1964) and the key symbolised the title of one of his best-known novels, *The Key above the Door*. The Oscar-winning film starring John Wayne and Maureen O'Hara was inspired by Walsh's story 'The Quiet Man', from his short-story collection, *Green Rushes*. The acclaimed film director John Ford read the story when it was first published in the *Saturday Evening Post* magazine in America on 11 February 1933. He secured the film rights shortly after, but it was 1952 before his iconic film was released. The character of Seán Thornton in the film (Seán Kelvin in the story) is based on a local man, Paddy 'Bawn' Enright, who was Maurice Walsh's neighbour in the parish of Ballydonoghue near Lisselton. The University of Limerick holds an original copy of the magazine as well as several handwritten and typescript drafts of the story, and The Seanchaí (Kerry Writers' Museum) in Listowel has a room dedicated to Maurice Walsh.

Fr Pat Moore is my guide once again as we head for a corner of Kerry I am traversing for the first time. Leaving *Lios Eiltin* (Eiltin's Fort) behind, we continue a short distance along the Ballybunion Road until we meet a signpost on the right indicating *Cnoc an Óir* (Hill of Gold). The hill is also known as *Cnoc an Fhómhair*. T. J. Barrington refers to it as *Cnoc an Air*, the Hill of the Slaughter, 'where Fionn and the Fiana [*sic*], with great killing, attempted to protect a greek [*sic*] princess fleeing from

husband and father.' The byroad climbs to the 879-foot summit
of the hill, where, Pat relates, a fire was lit in 1829 to spread the
news that Catholic Emancipation had been granted. The hill
still has a role in communication, but the twenty-first-century
beacon is a set of telecommunications masts and a humming
generator, which are the picture of ugliness. But, oh, what a
view! To the west is the broad expanse of the Shannon estuary,
Scattery and Hog Islands; on the far shore, the twin chimneys
of the Moneypoint electricity generation station; and, inland,
the white settlement of Killaloe in County Clare. On a fine
day you can see all the way to Galway Bay through binoculars.
To the east and south lie Ballybunion and the Cashen estuary
silvering its way to the Atlantic. And all is flat, mountainless, a
featureless plain so different from the mountainous terrain of
South Kerry.

Descending the hill, we follow the road westwards in the
direction of the Shannon estuary until we reach the village of
Asdee and, beyond it, a near-deserted beach called Littor (the
Latin word for shoreline). Littor, situated right at the edge of
the Shannon estuary, has not a shop or a bar or any sign of
commercial activity; it is pure unspoiled beach. The area around
here is said to have the highest concentration of All-Ireland
football medals in the county.

'The Shannon was the M1 motorway of Ireland,' according
to Pat, who grew up a stone's throw from Littor. 'The Celts, the
Vikings, the Cromwellian soldiers all used the Shannon to travel
right up into the heart of Ireland. They say Lislaughtin Abbey
was so beautiful in the month of May that the soldiers could
not destroy it, but when they were leaving, three old monks

rang the bell in happiness at being spared. The soldiers turned back and killed the three of them.' The Shannon was also used for access to North Kerry by settlers, including Captain Thomas Wren of Hinton in Cambridgeshire, who set up home in Littor House in the 1600s and was related to Sir Christopher Wren, the English architect who rebuilt London after the Great Fire of 1666.

Asdee is where the moving-statues phenomenon took hold in 1985. On 14 February locals reported seeing two statues in the church moving. Crowds arrived in the village to witness the alleged apparitions, and the phenomenon spread from there to a number of other Irish towns and villages, most famously, Ballinspittle in County Cork. While there has not been a stir out of the statues for some time, Asdee (*Eas Daoi*: the black waterfall) has another claim to fame. The Jesse James Tavern is a none-too-subtle hint. The famous outlaw's grandfather is said to have emigrated from nearby in the 1800s. According to Pat, Jesse James is not the only notorious American figure linked to Asdee: 'Bugsy Malone's ancestors were supposed to have come from between Asdee and Ballybunion. The Malones and the James family might have been pirates on the Shannon estuary.'

St Eoin's holy well is located about a mile and a half from the village of Asdee, in the townland of Snugboro, close to the Shannon. Local lore about the well holds that it moved to another field after someone washed their face in it.

Leaving Asdee for Ballylongford, we take the back road that leads towards the Shannon and the mud flats, which are a haven for migrating barnacle geese – a road not to be taken during spring tides because it floods. Carrig Island comes into sight and then Carrigafoyle Castle. This place feels like nowhere else in Kerry, like an ancient place that lodged in a slipstream of time. Carrigafoyle Castle, which dates from the late fifteenth century, was built by the chieftain Conor Liath O'Connor Kerry and incorporated a stretch of water in which, apparently, boats of up to 500 tons could be moored. *Carrig-a-foile* translates as the rock of the chasm. The castle was built beside Carrig Island, which is surrounded by the Shannon, so the chieftain was able to intercept boats going up the Shannon and take part of their cargo.

Sir William Pelham besieged the castle in 1580 during the Desmond Wars, and all the survivors were either hanged or put to the sword, including the Italian commander, sixteen Spaniards and fifteen Irish who numbered among the defenders. In *Discovering Kerry*, T. J. Barrington writes that this was the first effective use of artillery in Kerry and a 'neat combined naval and military operation', as guns were taken from naval vessels and mounted on the mainland, while ships from the Shannon bombarded the castle over Carrig Island. Despite other attacks during the Elizabethan and Cromwellian wars, the castle has stood the test of time well.

On the outskirts of Ballylongford Village is Aghavallen church where, in September 1851, the infant Horatio Herbert Kitchener was baptised. The churchyard dates back to the fourteenth century and contains the tombs of many of the landlord families of the area. In Aghavallen, the Irish and the Anglo-Irish slumber together, their tenure engraved on fine tombstones and simple grave markers. But the atmosphere was not always as easeful. Mark Humphrys reproduces on his website a letter written by a Miss R. Hill of Tarbert on 25 June 1898, in which she describes her attendance at Letitia Blennerhassett's burial there in 1876. She relates how Letitia's son, Joseph, had dug the grave in a certain location: 'Some parties named Twyford jumped into the grave and claimed the ground as theirs and would not allow her to be buried there so Joe had to make a new grave near the wall.'

Beside a wall of the ruined church, a plaque recalls two patriots of 1798 with the inscription, 'Eirí Amach 1798. In memory of William Leonard and Patrick Galvin, leaders of the United Irishmen in Ballylongford. Then here's their memory, may it be for us a guiding light.'

A little way down the road, Ballylongford, which translates as 'ford mouth of anchorage' (*Béal Átha Longfoirt*), has a link with another rebellion. One of the key figures of the Easter Rising of 1916, Michael Joseph O'Rahilly, also known by the self-styled title, The O'Rahilly, was born in the village on 22 April 1875. The son of a Ballylongford shopkeeper, The O'Rahilly was one of the founders of the Irish Volunteers in 1914 and its director of arms. An Irish-language enthusiast, he was a member of the governing body of the Gaelic League. He was educated in the exclusive Clongowes Wood College and married Nancy Brown on 15 April 1899. They honeymooned on the Grand Tour of Europe, then lived in New York and England, returning to Dublin in 1909. Although he opposed the Easter Rising because he felt it could only end in defeat, The O'Rahilly threw in his lot with the leaders on Easter Monday when he realised he was powerless to prevent the armed insurrection going ahead. 'Well, I've helped to wind up the clock, I might as well hear it strike,' he said as he joined the action. Another less quoted comment of his was, 'It is madness but it is glorious madness.'

The rebel Kerryman was cut down in a charge up Moore Street in Dublin on Friday 28 April 1916. Mortally wounded, he sheltered in a doorway on Sackville Lane, where he wrote a final message to Nancy on the back of a letter he had received from his son in the besieged GPO. That message was etched by artist Shane Cullen into the limestone and bronze plaque marking the lane, which has since been renamed O'Rahilly Parade:

> Written after I was shot. Darling Nancy I was shot leading a rush up Moore Street and took refuge in a doorway. While I was there I heard the men pointing out where I was and made a bolt for the laneway I am in now. I got more [than] one bullet I think. Tons and tons of love dearie to you and the boys and to Nell and Anna. It was a good fight anyhow. Please deliver this to Nannie O'Rahilly, 40 Herbert Park, Dublin. Goodbye Darling.

In Ballylongford the patriot's link with the village is commemorated in Finucane's Bar, which was his family home and where he was born upstairs: a life-sized portrait hangs in the bar. He is buried in the Republican Plot in Glasnevin Cemetery in Dublin.

Moving to more recent history, the village was linked to a national tragedy on 7 June 1996, when one of its native sons, Detective Garda Jerry McCabe, was shot dead in Adare, County Limerick, by members of the Provisional IRA during the attempted robbery of a post office. The death of the garda provoked an outraged reaction throughout Ireland. Among those who attended his funeral in Limerick was the crime journalist Veronica Guerin, who was gunned down by a member of a criminal gang outside Dublin only months later.

Ballylongford is the birthplace of one of Ireland's best-loved poets, Brendan Kennelly. The retired Trinity College professor, who was born in the village in 1936, holidayed in nearby Ballybunion for many years. The poet grew up in Kennelly's Bar, an institution in the life of Ballylongford to this day.

Still on the topic of verse, though on a much lighter note, the song 'Come Down from the Mountain Katie Daly' is said to have been composed in Ballylongford in the 1930s by a member of a travelling circus. Given that the village is at the edge of the great flat plain of Kerry, the source of the song's inspiration is perplexing to say the least.

Lady Lixnaw and Joyce

'There are two places to be in the world: Lixnaw and London.' This saying is attributed to a Lady Lixnaw of the Norman ascendancy family the Fitzmaurices, a dominant force in Kerry as lords, barons and earls from the 1100s to the 1700s. The last remaining walls of the Fitzmaurice mansion, Lixnaw Old Court, may be crumbling and shrouded in ivy, yet the ruin still has a cachet to hint at its history as a powerful Norman stronghold in Kerry over five centuries.

Lixnaw (*Leac Snámha*: the flagstone of the swimming) is located about ten kilometres south-west of Listowel. The River Brick flows beside the former country residence of the Fitzmaurices, who, in common with the gentry of their day, divided their time between London and their Irish estate; hence Lady Lixnaw's utterance. John Knightly, in his essay 'Lixnaw and the Earls of Kerry', described the ancient seat of the Fitzmaurice earls in Lixnaw as being largely the creation of Thomas Fitzmaurice, 1st Earl of Kerry (1668–1742), and his wife, Ann Petty (1672–1737), daughter of Sir William Petty, the Cromwellian adventurer. Knightly wrote that the 1st Earl 'maintained a lavish household at Lixnaw, befitting his status as de facto sovereign of Kerry'. Ann Fitzmaurice was credited by her grandson as being the inspiration behind the magnificence. He suggested that the use of pediments and projections and the general layout of Lixnaw evoked somewhat Clarendon House in London. 'By English standards, Lixnaw was probably unexceptional, but by Irish standards it was undoubtedly at the forefront of aristocratic taste.' The level of detail in John Knightly's article in the *Kerry Archaeological and Historical Society Journal* includes a minute listing of the wages of forty Lixnaw servants, who, in 1733, received a combined total annually of £274, 'a sum equal to the yearly income of a middling gentry family'.

Ballyduff historian Seán Quinlan writes that Old Court, which replaced an earlier castle, included a chapel decorated by artist John Souillard, with paintings copied from Raphael's cartoons at Hampton Court Palace. To the left of the house stood an octagonal building, the Cock House, which was used for the sport of cock fighting. Charles Smith, writing in 1750, described the beauty of the house standing 'agreeably on the river Brick, which is here cut into several pleasant canals that adorn its plantations and gardens'.

As the fortunes of the Fitzmaurices waned, so did their connection with Lixnaw, and by the time the 3rd Earl left the village in 1766, the house was already in decline. When the English travel writer Arthur Young dropped by ten years later, in 1776, the house was falling into ruin and the trees were being cut down. 'All is desolation and everything in ruins,' he lamented.

During its halcyon days, Lixnaw Old Court was linked to the family of one of the greatest Irish writers of all time, James Joyce. Valerie Bary wrote that Old Court was enlarged and improved in 1680. This chimes with an account in a biography of Joyce's father, John Stanislaus Joyce, recounting that one of his ancestors settled in the area in 1680. According to John Wyse Jackson and Peter Costello in their biography of Joyce's father, Seán Mór Seoighe (Big John Joyce) moved from County Galway (possibly travelling by sea) to work as a steward for William Fitzmaurice, the 19th Lord of Kerry. For his labours, he was given land nearby. The family trade of the Joyces of Connaught involved working with limestone – as lime-burners, stonemasons and builders. The biographers speculated that it was likely that Seán Mór was set in charge of the extensive building work on the banks of the Brick, and that he prospered in the position, along with his son, Risteard Caol (Richard the Thin). The following account of the mansion is given in the biography:

The thirteenth-century castle at Lixnaw had been demolished in about 1600, to be replaced by a Jacobean mansion called Lixnaw Old Court on the other side of the Brick River. As his new steward arrived, William FitzMaurice began to transform the house into a lavish modern residence and to tame the wilderness around it. Within a generation or two there would be built a mock ruin, which could be seen from the house, a building devoted to cockfighting, a family mausoleum and all the appurtenances of a grand country seat. The river was diverted to form scenic curves and a bathing place in the garden, and trees were planted along walks around the estate. Water parties were held and guests entertained lavishly.

Around 1750 some of the Lixnaw descendants of Seán Mór left Kerry to settle on Fitzmaurice land in Athlacca in County Limerick. From this branch of the family eventually sprang John Stanislaus Joyce, father of James Joyce, whose literary fame was to endure long after the lights and the lustre of Lixnaw Old Court dimmed and faded. The Lixnaw estate was eventually sold to the Hare family.

The demise of the beautiful house was unimaginable, however, in the era of Lady Ann Fitzmaurice, who had been described by the noted satirist Jonathan Swift as 'egregiously ugly, but perfectly well bred'. Given her contribution to Old Court, it is not beyond the bounds of possibility that Lady Anne was the Lady Lixnaw who uttered the words resonating down through the centuries long after the rooks and the ivy had taken over the home of the earls of Kerry, in the creation of which Joyce's ancestors played such a part.

The Forgotten Village

W hile the fortunes of The Cashen village have ebbed with the tide that races swiftly between the sand banks of the estuary, a rich legacy of memories has been handed down by the generations who lived off the once-bountiful salmon. The village lies on the southern bank of the mouth of the Cashen estuary, the single street of houses looking directly across to the world-famous links golf course at Ballybunion. A cul-de-sac road leads from the village of Ballyduff three miles away.

The warm smell of tar wafting up the seafront street in March was the signal that the fishing season was fast approaching. Tarring the new nets made from hemp or cotton was part of an entire ritual binding the life of the community with the salmon they harvested from the Cashen river where it rushed to meet the Atlantic. Donkeys were used up to the 1970s to pull the nets through special troughs filled with tar to make them waterproof. At the height of the fishing season, crews waiting their turn onshore to draw their nets along the 300-yard stretch of water passed the time in conversation or practising their dancing.

On a single day in 1963, an estimated 1,800 salmon were taken in about eight hours. Monofilament nets, new industry and pollution following agricultural development were among the factors that led to decimation of the priceless resource in the

1970s. The community has fought back, however, by promoting the estuary for recreational anglers fishing for bass and flounder.

When I revisited The Cashen in November 2013, there was not a boat to be seen. Horse boxes and jeeps were parked on the beach and youngsters cantered their ponies on the sand. A black cat sitting in the middle of the road at the street's end seemed incredulous at the prospect of moving to let the car past. Nearby, a black marble wall plaque commemorated the men of The Cashen who drowned while making their living from fishing.

On my previous visit in 1991, a few small black boats were moored out in the estuary. That April day Michael Rochford spelled out for me the malaise afflicting his homeplace, which he felt had become 'the forgotten village'. It was impossible to raise a crew because there were no fish. Barely four men were fishing that week, and only two salmon had been caught. 'The fishing won't come back, not in our lifetime,' Michael said prophetically.

The Cashen has a long tradition of producing fine singers and dancers. A succession of dancing teachers came to the dances in the old coastguard's house. The great 'Rambling House', where people gathered for entertainment, was that of Kate O'Brien, who was herself a beautiful singer. Seán Quinlan from Ballyduff counts The Cashen people as a 'jolly people', famed as singers and dancers and for their big 'wren dances' at Christmas time. 'My mother always said they were the best-dressed people going into Ballyduff church over the years. They didn't keep it [their money] when they made it.'

Since 1992 Seán has been building up the collection of the

North Kerry Museum, which is located a mile from Ballyduff on the Cashen Road and is a project of the Rattoo Heritage Society. It is in equal parts eclectic and fascinating: tools from two blacksmiths' forges, a set of double-spoked wheels from Colonel Rice's carriage, a thousand-year-old ladies' deerskin shoe retrieved from a bog and a Famine soup pot and ladle. There is the pulpit, Bible and baptismal jug from St Augustine's Church of Ireland church in Rattoo, which was transferred stone for stone in 1912 to Ballybunion where it serves as the town's public library. (After my museum visit, I travelled on to Ballybunion where I saw the church sitting there as naturally as if it was in its original location.) There is a 22-foot Early Bronze Age boat, discovered in The Cashen in the 1950s, carved from half an oak tree and estimated to be between 2,500 and 3,000 years old.

But this is not *the* boat. When I asked Seán to list some of the museum's most interesting items, he replied, 'We have the rarest thing of all: the Casement boat – and they're trying to take it off us.' The wooden boat, believed to be the one used by Casement and two companions to row from the German U-boat to Banna Strand in 1916, was acquired by the museum from the Ballyheigue Maritime Centre when it closed fourteen years earlier. Upstairs in the museum I get to see the boat and savour the experience of being so close to one of the most dramatic incidents in modern Irish history. The Department of Defence has been writing to Seán requesting the return of the boat 'known as the Casement boat'; the vessel had been stored in the Irish naval base at Haulbowline Island in Cork Harbour for many years until the link with Casement was suggested. He is philosophical about the eventual outcome: a window at least and, maybe more, will have to be removed if this boat is to float away from The Cashen.

My other call in Ballyduff that day was to Rattoo Round Tower on the edge of the village as you approach from Abbeydorney. Unfortunately it was swathed in scaffolding, but there was still access to the little abbey and graveyard adjoining it. Restoration work had been carried out on the abbey walls, and a large stone font rested on one of the windows. The tower, believed to be over 1,000 years old, is a remarkable feature rising out of the flat plains of North Kerry. It is one of thirteen perfectly preserved round towers out of a total of sixty-five towers remaining in Ireland. It is also the only round tower in Ireland with a sheela na gig carving. This is on the inside jamb of the north-facing window but can no longer be viewed because there are no stairs. A copy of it is, however, on view at Kerry County Museum in Tralee.

The term sheela na gig is said to come from the Irish, *Síle na gCíoch*, Julia of the breasts. The carvings portray the figure of a female squatting with her knees apart and her vulva exposed. The figures are often seen over church doors or windows and were believed to ward off evil spirits. But they were unlikely to ward off the depredations of the Viking raiding parties who were in the habit of coming up the Shannon and striking monastic settlements like the one at Rattoo. According to T. J. Barrington, the monastery was destroyed for the last time by the Irish in 1600 on the approach of the English under Wilmot.

Cornie Tangney

ornie Tangney used to leave his Christmas decorations up all year round; he did not believe in taking them down and going to the trouble of finding them the following year. 'I live alone,' he told me. 'There's only the dog, and he won't object to them.' I met Cornie (Cornelius) Tangney only once, about twenty-two years ago, in his home in Scartaglin, but I have spoken of him often since. He was a true original; the year-round decorations were only the half of it.

The son of a primary-school teacher, Cornie had tried a variety of careers by the time I called to his book-filled home in 1991: office work with the railway company CIÉ; ground technician with the Irish Air Corps in Baldonnel, County Dublin; attendant and trainee psychiatric nurse in St Finan's Hospital, Killarney; storekeeper and waterkeeper.

Scartaglin is located in the heartland of *Sliabh Luachra*, an area straddling the Kerry and Cork border famed for its traditional music and dancing. Cornie was as immersed in that rich culture as all his neighbours. He was a founder member of the Scartaglin Fleadh Cheoil in 1967. One of the first things he did as Fleadh secretary was to draft a letter inviting politicians to support the 'isolated hillside village'. There was one reply – a historic reply. It came in the form of a cheque for £5 from the then Finance Minister, Charles J. Haughey. The Fleadh was on the road.

If Cornie's place in the folklore of Scartaglin was not assured by then, it had good reason to be in the next decade. Some time in the 1970s Cornie, supposedly frustrated at delays in processing a social-welfare claim of his, blew up a disused shop in Castleisland in protest. He did, apparently, have the social-welfare office in Tralee in his sights, but abandoned that idea because it was too crowded. The shop at Mollie's Corner was empty, he gave adequate warning and nobody was hurt. The lore around the incident has grown with the years. Former Scartaglin publican Tom Fleming, who is now an independent TD, was told by one of the bystanders that Cornie warned them saying, 'If I was ye, I'd move out of here, there will be a bit of a bang going off in about ten minutes.'

When Cornie was sent to Mountjoy Prison in Dublin after the 'explosive incident' in Castleisland, the chaplain was a former neighbour of his, Fr John O'Connell from Counguilla, Scartaglin. Fr O'Connell, now retired in Bray, County Wicklow, describes Cornie as a 'super-intelligent guy, way above the average' and as a 'character who had unusual sayings and ways of putting things'. Someone once sympathised with Cornie by remarking, 'I hear ye buried yer father.' He replied, 'We had no choice, the man died.' On another occasion, he was ringing his former boss after he had lost his job. When the receptionist asked him who she should say was calling, he said, 'Ex-waterman Tangney'.

While he was in prison, Cornie made friends with the two other Kerrymen who were inmates. He 'flourished' there, taking charge of the prison library. Cornie's nephew, Gerald Borgeat, who grew up in England, wondered where his uncle was when he arrived for his summer holidays: 'I was told he was in Dublin learning the tailoring trade by which I understood he was sewing mail bags.'

Tom Fleming remembers Cornie for his great wit and IQ, which he rated as way above the ordinary. He believes that Cornie's ability was wasted, in that he did not seem to be able to settle in any job. He recalled that his tenure as a water bailiff on the Brown Flesk river was marked by a 'bit of flexibility'.

Cornie was pioneering in many ways. He invested in a cine camera in the 1950s and filmed the famous cycle race, the *Rás Tailteann*, from the back of a truck. He also wired the little hall where *céilithe* were held to raise money for the Fleadh Cheoil. A big open fire blazed in the hall every Thursday night when the dances were held. (The room survives as part of the Sliabh Luachra Cultural and Heritage Centre.) Those nights were emblazoned in Cornie's mind: 'Christ, that first winter of it was famous.'

The day I arrived at Cornie's front door to interview him for a newspaper article on Scartaglin, his black and white terrier, Latchico, raised a racket. The man of the house, dressed in a collar and tie, was sitting behind a little table with a marked air of expectancy; he could have been interviewing me for a job. From the word go I knew I was in the presence of a remarkable individual. In one corner he had a waterglass – a homemade invention for forecasting the weather through changes in the atmospheric pressure. These devices were in common usage about a century ago. He did not possess a television and he was none too happy at the practice of some Castleisland pubs having not one but two sets.

Not long after I met Cornie, he underwent cancer treatment in Dublin. Fr O'Connell visited him in St Luke's Hospital. The priest remembers a 'supernatural silence' when he broached the subject of how ill Cornie was. He asked him if he was at peace. 'Why wouldn't I be?' Cornie replied. That colourful son of Scartaglin died on 15 April 1992, but his funeral only took place on 6 July 1994, more than two years after he died, because he had donated his body to University College Cork for medical research. There was a great fanfare of the music he loved so well at his graveside.

The day I went to Scartaglin to meet Cornie, I also met two other outstanding villagers, blacksmith Paddy Casey and tailor John P. Brosnan, who have also passed since then. If there is a Heaven, Cornie is in great company, and the *craic* and the conversation are mighty.

The Headless Earl

Haggard, unwashed and unkempt, the 'outlaw' had been living the existence of a hunted animal when he was discovered by a search party in a forest encampment outside Tralee. One of his pursuers dashed into the dim and smoky hut and slashed him in the arm with a sword. Covering the gaping wound with his hand, the injured man cried out in pain, 'I am the Earl of Desmonde, save my life.' For the time being, the life of Gerald, the 16th Earl of Desmond, then a poor shadow of the once-powerful Norman lord he had been, was spared. It was decided to take him prisoner, but the reprieve was brief – a matter of hours.

Details of this final episode are given in *The Kerry Magazine* of July 1854, which reproduced a deposition given on 26 November 1583 of the manner in which the 'Erle of Desmond was pursued and slayne': 'On the night of 11 November, 1583, the last Earl of Desmond, at the age of sixty, was beheaded at Glanageenty Woods, Ballymacelligott, by one Daniel O'Kellye, motivated by the prospect of the reward of an annual pension of £20.' The nobleman's body was buried under an oak tree near where he had been slain but was reinterred eight weeks later at Kilnanama, Cordal, near Castleisland; his exact resting place in the graveyard is unknown. It is said that O'Kellye carried the head around in a bag for some time before it was sent to London and impaled on the Tower Bridge along with the heads of other traitors as a warning to anyone else tempted to rebel against Her Majesty Queen Elizabeth I. It was in fact taken to Castlemaine Castle before it was dispatched to London. O'Kellye himself was to make an unhappy trip across the water in due course. The benefits of his pension were short-lived; he was hanged at Tyburn for highway robbery (though I have wondered why he turned to crime when he had such a handsome pension).

The ill-fated Gerald, head of the Munster branch of the Geraldine family, was a rebel by default. The Crown, eager to move fresh English settlers into Desmond territory, was goading him into rebellion and had manufactured charges of conspiracy against him. The Geraldines, Italian in origin, had left Florence to live in Normandy around 910, and transferred from France to England with William the Conqueror in 1066. They were among the first waves of Normans who began to cross to Ireland in 1169.

Invaders at first, the Geraldines adopted the Gaelic way of life willingly; through intermarriage and the easy assimilation of the bardic culture and traditions they became 'more Irish than the Irish themselves'. Their fondness for literally 'sleeping with the enemy' did not exactly endear the Geraldines to their English overlords; tensions ebbed and flowed through the centuries. T. J. Barrington is compulsory reading for insights into the Geraldine Desmond dynasty, particularly his account of Katherine, daughter of the 4th Earl, who was at the centre of several scandals. She left home, having been caught in an affair with her brother, and took refuge with the Earl of Ormond, who raped her. 'She then regularised her position by poisoning his English countess and marrying him.' He also quotes a story from *Smith's History of Kerry* in which a young Desmond boy, who was about to be beheaded in 1468, along with his brother, 'besought the executioner not to hurt the boil that was on his neck'.

The relationship of Gerald, the final earl, with the monarchy had been mixed. He was knighted in 1558, but he also spent many years as a prisoner in the Tower of London. In January 1565, three weeks after the death of his first wife, Joan Butler, who had been twenty years his senior, he married Eleanor, who was described as an 'outstanding horsewoman'. Fearless in leading soldiers away from him in the woods while he was on the run, she is said to have dragged her badly injured husband into a river on one occasion to hide in the water until the search party moved on. While he was a prisoner in London, she kept charge of his army and collected the rent and sent money to London to make his life in the Tower less harsh.

According to the *Folk History of Blennerville*, Eleanor gave their only son and two others as a pledge of his loyalty when allegations of treason were being made against him. Desmond, however, still attacked the English camp at Rathkeale, saying that he 'owed the Queen no allegiance and would no longer yield her obedience'. At the close of 1579 he was proclaimed an outlawed traitor and became a wanted man for the next four years. His son was sent to England to be raised. When Patrick O'Haly, Bishop of Mayo, and Cornelius O'Rourke, a Franciscan, were executed, the earl retaliated in kind with atrocities.

His territory was convulsed in the Desmond Rebellion; his subjects endured untold suffering from war and famine as the lands were burnt and laid waste. The Vatican came to Desmond's aid on 13 September 1580, but the 600 soldiers, mostly Italian, were slaughtered without mercy in the military encampment of *Dún an Óir* at Smerwick Harbour in West Kerry. Barrington writes of successive raids on Kerry in 1580, including that of the Munster commander, Bourchier: 'Burning, killing and driving, he went from Castleisland to Dingle.'

The game was all but over when the fugitive earl was cornered like a wild animal in the woods at Glanageenty. The deposition of 1583 reveals how a cattle raid instigated by the earl and carried out by his few remaining followers led to his discovery. The earl remained in 'Doiremore' while his men went to Cahir-ni-fayhe west of Castle Gregory and stole the animals of Maurice Mac Owen and Robert Mac Edmund. 'In all they took forty cows, nine horses and other household stuff and they then stripped naked Maurice, his wife and children,' the account read.

The booty was to cost the earl his head when a search party 'followed the tract to Ballieore and on to Glanagyntie at Slieve Louchra, where they looked down and saw a fire beneath them'. After the attack, they all agreed to take turns in carrying the injured earl, but the game plan changed and Owen Mac Donel ordered him to be killed. According to Barrington, one of the O'Moriartys had carried the severely wounded earl along the glen but was unable to bring him up the other side, and the others refused to carry him. It was at this point that he was killed, even though he would have been worth twice as much alive.

The earl's death signalled the end of medieval Kerry and the beginning of Munster's colonisation by English settlers. Some 200,000 acres of his lands were granted to 'undertakers', who undertook to plant the lands with English and Protestant farmers. Among the family names that entered the lexicon of Kerry from 1584 onwards were those of Herbert, Denny, Conway, Blennerhassett, Chute, Crosbie and Browne. According to Barrington, the earl's widow, Eleanor, was pardoned on condition that she renounced all claims to the estate. 'She and her five children for some time lived in great poverty until in 1587 Elizabeth granted her a pension of £200 a year.'

Kerry's Sherwood Forest

Kerry has an abundance of walking routes delivering the purest experience of nature in peaceful surroundings, but few can rival the Glanageenty Walk, where a rich concentration of history and compelling stories complement the varied landscape of the wooded valley. Located just off the N21 Tralee to Castleisland road, a short drive behind O'Riada's Bar, Glanageenty is compared to Sherwood Forest because it served as a hiding place for fugitives with experiences dramatic enough to inspire a brace of feature films. The Gaelic version of Glanageenty is *Gleann na gCaointe*, which may translate either as the Valley of Mourning or the Valley of the Fairies.

In the Desmond survey of 1584, this area was described as one of the wildest and most remote parts of Munster. Glanageenty is literally a walk through history – right from the starting point. At the edge of the tree-fringed roadway linking the lower and upper parking areas, a limestone monument commemorates Gerald FitzGerald, the last Earl of Desmond, who was beheaded at Glanageenty on 11 November 1583. His head was taken as a trophy to London for display on Tower Bridge to dissuade other would-be traitors to the Crown; his body was buried at Kilnanama Graveyard near Castleisland. The monument was erected on 11 November 1983 by the Kerry Archaeological and Historical Society to mark the 400th anniversary of FitzGerald's death.

Having meditated on such cheerful happenings, walkers can choose between two routes looping along the valley floor and rising to the ridges above. Allow yourself between one and a half and two hours. The route is well signposted, and there is an excellent series of information boards. If you have a good level of fitness, opt for the longer Lenihan's Loop, which has one final, sharp ascent rising to 900 feet and an incomparable panorama of Kerry's mountain line stretching from Mount Brandon on the ocean's edge to Carrantuohill in the MacGillycuddy Reeks and over to the Paps near Rathmore; you may even glimpse Clara across the Cork border on a fine day.

The existence of this walk is due chiefly to the generosity of local landowners, John and Mary Lenihan, Francie Lenihan and the descendants of brothers John and Richard Bernard. Their openness to granting access to the public was the basis for a partnership with Coillte, North and East Kerry Development and Fáilte Ireland to develop the walk, which was officially opened in 2012. Prior to that, John Lenihan, a mountain runner with a slew of international titles to his name, used to run the woods on training sessions with his friends. 'Their love of the landscape sowed the seed to create the loop walk,' John said.

The Lenihans have a direct family link to Stephen Fuller, the sole survivor of a Civil War landmine atrocity on 6 March 1923 known as the Ballyseedy Massacre. Badly wounded and fearing for his life, Fuller escaped to a local house from where he was smuggled to the mountain valley. John relates:

My grandmother, Annie Boyle, had to get out of bed that night and give her bed to Stephen. She was an only girl and had a room to herself. He had horrific flesh wounds. She was describing how the gravel had to be removed from his body.

After a short time with the Boyles, the injured man was moved to a neighbouring farm owned by the Herlihy family. He recovered and went on to represent North Kerry as a TD in later years.

Not far from John and Mary Lenihan's farm and still on the ridge top, the loop passes the site of a Desmond castle of which no trace remains but which is part of the local history, as John explains:

> There was always a flat green area known as the castle field on our farm. The road up to my house would go right through it. That castle field does tie in with maps where a Desmond castle is marked. When we were digging there in the 1970s to make the road there was fierce local interest as to what was going to be dug up as the road was made, but nothing showed up.

Where the track rising through the woods briefly crosses the main road, the water pouring over a nearby rockface was believed to originate from a holy well and to hold special powers. This was the main route for people from Ballymacelligott travelling to the bogs of Lyreacrompane to cut turf. They believed that if their horse drank from the well in the morning it would not need water again until its homeward journey in the evening. Another rockface 200 metres south of the little waterfall is known as Blackbird's Rock.

After a descent into a section of the valley floor through which a swift stream sings, the route passes the ruins of the humble home of Seán Thaidgh Óig, a mountain recluse who gave shelter to another fugitive, this time on Good Friday 1916. Captain Robert Monteith was one of two men who landed at Banna Strand with Sir Roger Casement, having travelled from Germany by U-boat to support the Easter Rising with German arms. Nothing went according to plan, and Monteith ended up a wanted man in dire need of the shelter of the Glanageenty oak woods. He was also helped by another Lenihan family in the valley.

Aside from the sojourns of these troubled visitors, life went on as normal for the many valley dwellers, among them the Bourke family, whose homestead is commemorated by one of the many information boards along the walk.

In recent times, Glanageenty and neighbouring areas have produced athletes who have excelled in international competitions. John Lenihan is just one of several fleet-footed runners from the area. In 1991 he trained in this valley before travelling to the Matterhorn in Switzerland to become the first Irishman to win the world title for mountain running. Athlete Tom McCarthy and cyclist Dan Aherne, who also had stellar international careers, have been honoured along the walkway by having two footbridges named after them.

The unique character of the valley's walking routes has encouraged local businesses to sponsor not only the information boards, but also benches and tables at scenic points overlooking vistas of Tralee Bay and other views and in silent pockets of the woodland. As well as recounting historical events, the boards describe the flora and fauna and some of the lore going with them. For instance, the bark of the black sally was boiled and used as a poultice to ease pains and strains, while salkin, the liquid inside the bark, was used to ease headaches.

The return stretch of the walk leads through a former forest floor where oak, hazel and mountain ash saplings are springing up between tree stumps and the purple heather and yellow gorse bed brightly together. A vista of the Slieve Mish Mountains and Tralee Bay lies ahead, and a cast of characters remain behind in the trees that were once their refuge and their homes.

The Town of the Rose

The most common version of the story behind the ballad 'The Rose of Tralee' is that William Pembroke Mulchinock, son of a wealthy merchant family, fell in love with a servant girl, Mary O'Connor, who worked in his family home, Cloghers House, during the nineteenth century. The story goes that Mary's ravishing beauty did not win her any favour with the parents of her noble lover, who were not impressed by her humble origins in, supposedly, Brogue Lane, part of a warren of laneways in the town centre. William Mulchinock married someone else and emigrated to America. Returning years later to find that Mary had died of tuberculosis (or a broken heart depending on the version), he wrote the love song that has become Tralee's anthem.

There are, however, dissenters to this creed of the rose. Local historian Peter Locke wrote in the *Kerry's Eye* newspaper in 2002 that the ballad was composed by Mordaunt Spencer in about 1850 and that the melody was by C. W. Glover. Locke further gives an account of an Edward Mulchinock who 'stood as father' to a child born outside of marriage to a servant girl, Ann Sullivan, in 1848. 'Was it from the association between the couple that the love story surrounding the Rose of Tralee began?' he asked. Whatever truth lies at the heart of the mystery of the rose, it is a certainty that the ballad inspired the founding of the annual Rose of Tralee Festival (now the Festival of Kerry) in 1958.

One of the highlights of the festival is a Disneyesque parade of floats ferrying the Roses down Denny Street towards the Ashe Memorial Hall, on the steps of which the newly crowned Rose of Tralee is introduced to the cheering crowds. The fabric of Denny Street has changed little since it was developed in 1828. Its houses are characterised by elegant fanlights and flights of steps, remnants of the genteel and prosperous era when Tralee, served by the sea port of Blennerville, was booming as a centre of trade and commerce. But if we peel back a few centuries, this Georgian area presents a very different face, that of medieval Tralee. This world is vividly conjured up by Tralee historian Russell McMorran and his brother, Clare McMorran, in their book, *Tralee: A Short History and Guide to Tralee and*

Environs. (The book is beautifully illustrated by Clare McMorran's sketches.)

The key figure to emerge among the Anglo-Norman invaders who founded medieval Tralee was John FitzThomas FitzGerald, who built the Great Castle and, according to Russell McMorran, 'used Tralee as a base from which to build up the greatest Anglo-Norman lordship in Munster'. Under his stewardship a grant of borough status was granted to Tralee, which was dominated by the Great Castle standing on the site of present-day Denny Street on the bank of the Big River, which now runs underground. The earls of Desmond, who descended from FitzThomas FitzGerald, fell out of favour with the British monarchy and became embroiled in the Desmond War (1579–83). The rebellion resulted in Tralee being burnt several times and the obliteration of practically everything the Desmonds had put their stamp on. Exit the Geraldines. (To regain that sense of Geraldine Tralee, visit its reconstruction at Kerry County Museum in the Ashe Memorial Hall.)

Russell McMorran pinpoints the birth of modern Tralee to the plantation of Munster with these new settlers. 'In 1587, the newly-created 6,000 acre "Seignory of Traly" was granted by Queen Elizabeth to a well-connected English adventurer, Edward Denny, with whose family the fortunes of the town were to be closely linked for the ensuing three hundred years,' he wrote. Denny, a son of one of Henry VIII's courtiers, brought over English settlers, including the Blennerhassett, Chute and Morris families. Not everything ran smoothly for the new wave of settlers. The Cromwellian forces paid a visit in 1652, destroying the Dominican Priory of Holy Cross; the order had been introduced to Tralee in 1243 by the Geraldines, who continued as their patrons. The Dominicans returned to Tralee in 1861. Holy Cross church was blessed and opened beside Day Place on 14 September 1871. There is still a strong devotion to the prior and martyr Father Thaddeus Moriarty, who was hanged in Killarney in October 1653. Today, the original site of the priory, which stood on five acres of ground, corresponds roughly with the Abbey Car Park, a minute's walk from Tralee's Town Square.

Fast forward to December 2013 and to Denny Street, where I am standing beside the Pikeman Memorial with Mike O'Donnell, my guide for a walking tour of the town. Mike points across the street to the Grand Hotel, where the name 'Samuels' appears on the façade. He explains that the notorious landlord's agent, Samuel Murray Hussey, once had his office in the building. Hussey remarked in his memoir, which was published in 1904, 'I do not say so much about Tralee being able to support 160 liquor shops because there is a little shipping, but how Cahirsiveen can enable fifty publicans to thrive is a melancholy mystery to me.' The Grand Hotel was also the base for Tralee's first telephone exchange, which, Mike tells me, was the size of a grand piano.

The Pikeman, erected to honour those who fought in the 1798 rebellion, is a moving statue of sorts because it has been located on two different sites in Denny Street during its eventful history. The original statue was unveiled on 21 September 1902 by Maud Gonne, the English-born revolutionary for whom the poet W. B. Yeats had an unrequited love and wrote many poems. Tralee man Tomás Slattery has a personal interest in the statue because his grandfather, Thomas Slattery, Chairman of Tralee Urban Council, was present at the unveiling in 1902. To mark the occasion, Maud Gonne was presented with a silver trowel inscribed by jeweller P. Crowley of Castle Street, Tralee. 'He described Maud Gonne's beauty as the same as Joan of Arc,' Tomás said.

The Slattery family was very involved in the fight for Irish freedom. The family home at Nos 10 and 11 Rock Street was burnt down on 1 November 1920 by the British 'Black and Tans', as they were 'affectionately' known. The Tans toppled the Pikeman from its plinth in April 1921 and smashed it into pieces on the street. The replacement, located further up the street, was completed by Albert Power (1881–1945), who is also responsible for the statue of Pádraic Ó Conaire on Eyre Square in Galway.

When the new memorial was unveiled on 24 June 1939, Maud Gonne MacBride – she had married in the meantime – did the honours again. Tomás, who was seven years old at the time, shared the following vivid recollection of the aged revolutionary: 'My father got an invitation onto the platform but I refused to go up on it because I thought Maud Gonne was a witch. She was dressed in a huge black hat. She had a black veil over her face and a long black coat.'

On a more contemporary note, an overenthusiastic reveller scaled the statue during the Rose of Tralee Festival in 1994. The crowd shouted at him to jump, but he was eventually retrieved by the fire service.

My tour with Mike O'Donnell was meant to begin from Casement Railway Station, named after the patriot Roger

Casement, who came ashore on Banna Strand near Ardfert in Easter 1916 as part of his abortive attempt to bring German arms to support the uprising. However, because of heavy rain, we began at the top of Ashe Street, where the Dingle train used to pass on its way through town to Blennerville.

The Big River is still visible beside Dunnes Stores, but it now flows under Ashe Street, previously Nelson Street. A bridge used to cross the river directly opposite St John's Church of Ireland church, which dates back to the 1830s and was built on the site of a medieval church. The Bible of the Kitchener family of North Kerry is held at the church, whose gates originally came from the Talbot-Crosbie estate.

Further down Ashe Street on the left is the imposing Tralee Court House (1835), which is fronted by a pair of Crimean cannon commemorating Kerrymen who fought in colonial wars in China and India. Across the street from the courthouse is the Kerry Protestant Hall (1863), which has the unusual feature of a chimney set to the front of the building. At the corner of Church Street is the attractive red-brick Law Chambers.

Sheltering from the rain further down Church Street, Mike and I stood in the doorway of No. 8, which was the last working forge in Tralee. After the smith, Mick Griffin, had given up shoeing horses, he moved across the street to a workshop where he continued his ironwork, which included making *sleáns* for cutting turf. Mick's forge had been well placed, because Tralee's creamery was located here, just off Church Street and in the shadow of the Church of Ireland. When Mike O'Donnell gives schoolchildren a tour, he tells them that the creamery queue, which extended into Ashe Street, was the equivalent of

Facebook in the way that the farmers passed on news to each other and carried it home to their parishes.

Church Street leads into Barrack Square on either side of which were the towering grain stores of Latchford's and McCowan's, where barley was dried and processed. There is a plaque on one of the shopfronts, 'J. Madden Flour and Meal Merchant 1860'. Milk Market Lane continues off the Square; one of its offshoots is Broguemakers' Lane (bróg is the Irish for shoe). On this street also was the site of the first house occupied by Presentation Sisters when they came to Tralee on 9 July 1809. No. 13 Milk Market Lane was the home of Mick Grady, a gifted plasterer whose work is seen in many of the house fronts.

When I wrote about this area in 1991, one of the residents I spoke to was Seamus O'Mahony, who ran a sweet shop and whose family had lived there since 1912. Seamus's explanation for the name of a nearby section of lane was that it was called Pye Lane after a Scotsman who had introduced electricity locally. The common interpretation was that it was called Pie Lane because of the pie-makers who fed all the country people who came to the fairs held beside Milk Market Lane. Seamus remembered men with pikes and shovels coming over the Short Mountain from Killorglin and Castlemaine to the hiring fair. One of their stipulations was three days off for the Puck Fair. In those days, nearly every house in the locality was an eating house and a lodging house for the horse dealers and the jobbers.

Pye Lane, and another laneway, Barrack Lane, lead out to the busy shopping thoroughfare of the Mall, where, on the right-hand side, the decorative red brickwork of the Phoenix Building can be seen high above the street. This shop was owned by the Revington family and was regarded as the Brown Thomas of Tralee in its day. Revington's actually did become part of Brown Thomas in 1965 when the Dublin company bought the business; it continued to trade as Revington's but was sold to Power Supermarkets (Pat Quinn) just a few years later.

Behind the Mall is the Square where the town's main markets were held. There is a plaque in memory of one of the original stallholders, Judith Bron (1725–1835), who lived to be 110 years of age. On the south side of the Square, Hogan's shop was once the home of the Thompson family where Archbishop Thomas Croke (1824–1902) holidayed as a child.

Dominick Street leads from the Square through the Abbey Car Park again, site of the original Dominican Priory, and onto Day Place, an attractive terrace of Georgian houses built in 1805 by Judge Robert Day (1745–1841). Near the front door of Holy Cross church at the end of Day Place is a beautiful old holy water font, which is believed to have originated in the old priory. The community of Dominicans is still in possession of a silver chalice presented to the order in 1651.

Other places worth visiting in Tralee include Rock Street, famed for its footballing heroes. The street's Castle Bar takes its name from Castle McEllistrim, the ruins of which stood there until the middle of the 1800s. Rock Street's Urban Terrace is known as the 'Street of Champions' because of its unique record in Gaelic football: players reared in the twenty houses brought twenty-two senior All-Ireland medals home to Kerry between them: Micko Doyle, Jimmy Gorman, Billy Landers, John Joe

Landers, Tim Landers, Gal Slattery (the Austin Stacks club) and Thady Gorman (the John Mitchels club).

Rock Street has been immortalised in a poem, 'The Boys from the Top of the Rock', written by the late Ned Drummond, a resident of Urban Terrace. The following is the opening verse:

If you want to be happy the rest of your life
Come up to the Top of the Rock
It's the grandest spot in Ireland
And full of the rare old stock
No matter what your past may be
If you haven't the price of a block
They'll never see you down and out
Above at the Top of the Rock.

Blennerville, the old port for Tralee, and a major embarkation point for emigration, takes its name from Sir Rowland Blennerhassett, who developed it in the 1780s to include the windmill which is now a visitor's centre. The opening of the Tralee Ship Canal in 1846 enabled ships to sail right up as far as the Brandon Hotel and was one of the factors that led to the decline of Blennerville. The windmill itself had its own tale of tragedy. Sir Rowland was married to Millicent Yielding of Bellview, County Limerick, and she was killed by a blow from one of the windmill sails in about 1802. The story goes that she walked out onto the balcony shortly after the mill was built; the wind blew her off her feet and into the blades.

Dynamite in the Night

The force of the explosion shook Edenburn House to its foundations and blew a hole in the building's 3-foot-thick wall. The blast, caused by dynamite detonated in the basement, was heard four miles away in Castleisland. Windows were blown out and glass shattered in two greenhouses over 100 yards from the house. The ground-floor area was smashed to pieces and the window frames and shutters were 'shivered into atoms'. Sixteen people were sleeping in the house when the explosion ripped through it between 4 a.m. and 4.30 a.m. on 30 November 1884. Among them were three policemen assigned for a number of years to protect the land agent, Samuel Murray Hussey, and his family. This account is culled from reports in three newspapers, *The Manchester Guardian*, *The Times* and the *Cork Constitutional*.

Sam Hussey, as the notorious land agent was known, gave a largely humorous account of the attempt on his life when he came to write his memoirs many decades later. He wrote that in the aftermath of the explosion he said to his wife, "'My dear, we can have a quiet night at last, for the scoundrels won't bother us again before breakfast." … And I can solemnly testify that within ten minutes of that observation I was fast asleep, and never woke till I was called.' Laconic is a word used to describe his delivery more than once in the course of the Edenburn episode. 'Dynamite and badly managed' was the explanation he offered at the scene. He described the appearance of his brother, John, 'with a candle in one hand and a revolver in the other, with which he was rubbing his sleepy eyes'. His daughter, Florence, later quoted him as saying, 'Don't be uneasy about a mere dynamite explosion; it's like an Irishman's pig, you want it to go one way and it invariably goes in the other.'

Hussey, who was the son of a barrister, ends his account with one 'delicious incident': 'the local branch of the Land League in Castleisland refused to pay any reward to the dynamiters because we had not been killed'. He did not seem over-fond of Castleisland, declaring that 'almost anyone could have been shot at Castleisland if a sovereign were offered, for they cared no more for human life than a rat'.

The Sam Hussey who emerges from the pages of *The Reminiscences of an Irish Land Agent* has a self-deprecating wit and a Wildean talent for aphorisms. This entertaining style, coupled with an unwavering self-regard as 'the poor man's friend', serves to distract the reader from the fact that he was one of the most loathed individuals in the Kerry of his day. Killarney author Joseph O'Connor does not spare Hussey in an account of a meeting with him in Aghadoe. 'Even in his old age in a bath chair he was a dominating, repellent brute,' he wrote. Describing Hussey as a 'lonely old man', the author relates: 'His sons had fled from his domineering rule; his favourite daughter had just run away with his coachman.'

In his memoir, Hussey meets his critics head on, including the 'ink-slinging' variety, and does not flinch from quoting their worst vitriol. Take, for instance, a letter from one Daniel O'Shea in the *New York Table* in 1880, referring to 'that ruthless

Sam Hussey' and stating that 'If all Ireland were searched for a similar despot he would not be found. He is a regular anti-Christ and Orangeman at heart, and, in fact, he acts as agent for all the bankrupt landlords in Kerry.' Hussey admits to having 'received' the rents of one-fifth of the whole of Kerry 'in the worst of times', his payment being 5 per cent of all he collected. He goes on to say, 'Perhaps what I am proudest of, was being called in an address in Kerry "the poor man's friend", for it is what I have always striven to be.' He claims to have been responsible for only ten evictions in six years among 2,000 tenants. He once told Lord Kenmare, 'Popularity and getting in money were never on the same bush.'

For a man supposedly on the side of the poor, there were a hell of a lot of people out to get him. After the curious incident of the dynamite in the night, the Hussey family moved to Killarney, where they leased Aghadoe House (now an An Óige hostel) from Lord Headley. Here there were five policemen constantly present, two on sentry duty all night. At about 2 a.m. one morning, shots were heard in the woods and around the house, supposedly to lure the police out so that the house and its occupants could be 'disseminated' once again 'by the gentle and persuasive influence of dynamite'. Signs of blood were found on the road towards Beaufort the next morning. All this Sam Hussey relates with the same dry wit that he employs in quoting a friend, Lord Morris, pointing him out saying, 'That's Jack the Snipe who provided winter shooting for the whole of Kerry, and not one of them could wing him.'

Hussey credits a *Daily Telegraph* editor with ascribing the nickname 'Woodcock Hussey' to him, 'because he was never hit, though often shot at'. While the land agent's perspective is understandably one-sided, it is nonetheless a riveting social document, delivering insights into a range of aspects of Kerry life. Among the most shocking of his descriptions are those of the atrocities visited on tenants by 'their own' for paying rent during the Land War when payments were being withheld. He recounts how two tenants, Cronin and O'Keeffe, came to him in Killarney in November 1881 to say they would be glad to pay their rent only that they were afraid they would be shot. To Hussey's 'lasting regret' he told them there would be no fear of that. A week later, all the flesh on the lower part of O'Keeffe's legs was shot away and two Cronins were shot in the leg and the body. He describes another form of punishment called 'carding', consisting of 'a wooden board with nails in it being drawn down the naked flesh of a man's face and body'.

Despite several attempts on his life, receiving over 100 threatening letters and a lifestyle in which he regularly placed a revolver beside his fork on the dinner table, Sam Hussey expresses a great affection for Kerry. He relates how his sister Mary died in Bath when he was born. 'It was her health which prevented me from being by birth what I am at heart, a Kerry man,' he wrote. Dingle, I am afraid, must claim Hussey, for it was there he was brought as a three-month-old baby and it was there the Hussey family had settled in 'very early times' – his grandfather, John Hussey, lived in the town. And Sam Hussey did not believe he ever went out of Kerry – 'he had too much sense'.

He began to farm 60 acres in Dingle in 1843, using the scientific system he had learned in Scotland, but he did not consider it big enough. 'Had I been able to obtain a reasonably large farm near Dingle, I should never have become a land agent,' he said. No doubt, some other personage would have fallen in for the job of 'receiving' the rents of Kerry, but would he have left behind such an eloquent yet jaundiced account of the Kerry of his day?

Brosnan and Sheehy, Peacebrokers

(by Jimmy Darcy)

I reland in the 1920s was a country wracked and almost ruined by the travails of the misnamed 'Great War' and our own War of Independence, and even more so by the partisan and bitter divisions of the Civil War, wars that grew bloodier and more horrendous as they shrank from global significance to local importance. Recruitment for the First World War was a controversial topic in Kerry, but plenty of Kerrymen marched into bombs and bullets and the dreaded mustard gas with the Munster Fusiliers and their like.

It is a moot point whether the War of Independence started with the Easter Rising in Dublin's GPO or whether it was an inevitable ongoing chapter in an 800-year-old story. What is undeniable is that there were awful brutalities on both sides, and

Kerry in particular was a hotbed of martial as well as political resistance. However, while it is true that the hearts and minds of most Kerry people were with the IRA, they were also devoted to Gaelic football.

The Gaelic Athletic Association (GAA) was a youngster in Kerry at that time. Rowing and athletic traditions went back hundreds of years, and rugby and cricket were well established, whereas Maurice Davin's hybrid of the old game of 'caid' and rugby had been in existence only since 1884. Kerry won its first All-Ireland in 1891 in the sport of hurling, with an amalgamated team from Ballyduff, but then football took over. The county won its first All-Ireland Senior Football Championship in 1903, beating Kildare after two replays that captured huge public attention. Among their biggest stars were Killarney's Dick Fitzgerald and Tralee's Austin Stack; both men were leaders on the field – and later leaders in the IRA's fight for Irish independence.

When the War of Independence ended, it led to an internal struggle even more bitter and vicious. The Treaty settlement terms of December 1921, particularly partition, were viewed by many IRA members as an unacceptable compromise that tainted the legitimacy of the new Free State. The Civil War left the Free State government victorious but in a shaky position, and internment of former dissident republicans, the vast majority of whom had fought in the War of Independence as IRA members, was viewed as an unsavoury but necessary option. It was a bad mistake.

In Kerry, Austin Stack, Humphrey Murphy and Moss Galvin were interned. All three were hugely significant public figures in the GAA, both as administrators as well as players, and Kerry withdrew its participation in the 1922 All-Ireland championship in protest. In the following year, many of the Kerry team had been released and the county reached the 1923 All-Ireland Final against Dublin, who won by 1–5 to 1–3 fair and square.

One man who couldn't take part in the 1924 campaign was John Joe Sheehy of John Mitchels GAA Club, Tralee: there was still a warrant out for his arrest. Fellow die-hard and unrepentant republican Joe Barrett took Sheehy's place in the full-back's jersey. Con Brosnan played midfield. The great fielder had been born in Newtownsandes, lived for a while in Newtownclarke and eventually ended up in Moyvane – he never moved, but the town changed its name three times during those often confused and troubled times. Brosnan had been a highly admired republican leader during the War of Independence but he had stood by the Free State during the Civil War. He was now a captain in the Irish Army and the man whose duty it was to capture John Joe Sheehy.

Kerry had already beaten Tipperary comfortably in the 1924 championship, as was expected. Cork were lying in the long grass waiting for them, and everyone inside Cork and outside it knew that they had good players.

Munster semi-final. Kerry versus Cork. A young man steps out from the crowd onto the field of players. Whispers run through the crowd, wild rumours. Then John Joe Sheehy casually takes off his jumper and takes his place, apparently oblivious to a sudden standing ovation from the crowd, Cork and Kerry alike. Kerry win and win well, 4–3 to 2–1. Sheehy is outstanding. Instead of going into the dressing room after the match, he disappears into the crowd again.

It transpires that Joe Barrett and Con Brosnan had brokered the truce together, a truce that had a far deeper significance than any football match – even one against Cork. Kerry won the Munster Final against Clare, saw off Mayo in the All-Ireland semi-final and beat Dublin to lift the Sam Maguire, but it is not that All-Ireland Final, which Kerry won by 0–4 to 0–3, that remains the shining memory of that championship.

Years later, in 1931, Joe Barrett, as the nominee of county champions John Mitchels GAA Club, had the right to the captaincy of a Kerry team going for three in a row. Instead of taking the honour himself, he nominated Con Brosnan. The Moyvane maestro went on to lift the Sam Maguire.

Gabriel Fitzmaurice, the great North Kerry poet, has written a beautiful poem, 'Munster Football Final 1924', celebrating that famous meeting of Brosnan and Sheehy on the field of play instead of the field of war. I will borrow from his work for the final words on the matter:

Nothing polarises like a war,
And, of all wars, a civil war is worst;
It takes a century to heal the scars
And even then some names remain accursed.
The tragedies of Kerry, open wounds –

John Joe Sheehy on the run in 'twenty-four
The Munster Final in the Gaelic Grounds:
There's something more important here than war.

A Manner of Speaking

Many moons ago, I was working behind the counter of my family's grocery shop in Killarney when an elderly woman came in and announced, 'I went down to the International [Hotel] to get some string to tie the turkey's legs, and they gave me enough to hang all the cows in Kerry.' Another elderly customer was a master at materialising at your elbow without warning when some private business was being discussed; his nickname was 'Steal-upon-Birds'. At Listowel Writers' Week in more recent times, the news that a wealthy male author had won the big cash prize for his novel provoked the following reaction from a local: 'That's like rubbing lard into a fat pig's arse.' Puck Fair, the Killorglin festival at which a goat is crowned king every August, provides us with a beautiful image for the waning light at the start of autumn: 'Puck Fair Night the tailor lights his candle.' A few months later, the waxing light of January evenings is called 'the cock's step'.

This natural inventiveness with language is a gift celebrated inside Kerry and beyond, whether for a colourful turn of phrase or an Irish word wending its way into common speech. Often, our individualised manner of speaking is unconscious; it can take the reaction of an outsider to make us realise that our idiom or dialect is unique. For instance, a common phrase like 'the potatoes went against them', meaning that the crop failed, can be a source of wonder to an outsider. The richness of the spoken word in Kerry owes much to the fact that people have been drawing from both the Irish and English languages down through the generations; the term 'Hiberno-English' has been coined to define the mellifluous meeting of two tongues.

Patrick Weston Joyce from Limerick, writing in 1910, traced the influence of Old English and Scottish back to the Anglo-Norman invasion in the twelfth century, and to Elizabethan colonists who arrived from the sixteenth century onwards. He wrote:

> There was give and take in every place where the two peoples and the two languages mixed. And so the native Irish people learned to speak Elizabethan English – the very language used by Shakespeare; and in a very considerable degree the old Gaelic people and those of English descent retain it to this day.

My own experience is that regions of Kerry where the Gaelic tongue lingered longer, for instance Iveragh, have retained a higher usage of Irish words in day-to-day conversation. But as the gap grows wider between the original generations of Irish speakers and their descendants, I believe that our rich store of verbal imagery is dwindling. Here I will present a selection of some of the best colloquialisms used by people in the generations before mine and also the Irish words and phrases which have been passed down to us and still persist to a certain degree. Many of the expressions are inspired by agriculture and farm stock, with the pig and the hen providing some of the best sayings. (My father once pushed a cup of 'hospital tea' away from him, saying, 'A pig wouldn't face it.') Here is a selection with explanations where they may be needed:

He knows as much about that as a pig knows about a white shirt.

You're making a pig's arse of it. (You are making a mess of it.)

What would you expect from a pig but a grunt.

As scarce as hens' teeth. (Hens have no teeth.)

She's no hen laying out. (A sensible, cautious woman.)

She's a laying hen. (A woman with a job.)

He'd put legs under eggs. (He exaggerates.)

I've seen hens looking out of better. (His car is not impressive.)

He would tell lies as fast as a cock would crow.

The older the goat, the giddier.

Older generations had little tolerance for those who had ideas above their station. Phrases referring to such people included: 'He has a great welcome for himself.' If one poor person was criticising another, the phrase was, 'A penny halfpenny looking down on a halfpenny.' My own favourite in this genre, given to me by my late aunt, Nancy Joy, is: 'High-minded, like Bradley's gander that got up on the ditch to die.'

Asking a person how they are getting on in Kerry can provoke a variety of responses:

Pulling the Devil by the tail.

Ara, I'm only *strácáiling*.

Keeping the good side out like the cracked jug on the dresser.

If I were any better, they'd put me in a film.

The word *strácáil* means to struggle; it gives the impression of a person barely able to drag themselves along. Though *ara* is widely used in Kerry; other forms of the interjection are *wirra* or *irra*. They are derived from *A Mhuire*, Mary, a form of address to the Mother of God.

One of the old sayings for telling a person to be quiet is, 'Hauld your *whisht*' or simply, '*Whisht*, will you.' It is derived from the Gaelic word *tost*, silence. An admonishment to keep a secret is 'Keep that under your cap.' Someone who had imparted a piece of information in a spirit of one-upmanship would say, 'Put that in your pipe and smoke it.'

Unlike the trend of today to make a virtue out of being thin, being underweight attracted negative comment in the past; maybe this was a hangover from too many years of starvation. Sharp features came in for ridicule also:

He's like a pull-through for a rifle.

He could sleep on a clothes line.

His jaw would cut tabaccy for you.

He has a nose like the point of a rifle for shooting fleas.

On the other hand, common euphemisms for putting on weight include 'He got strong' and 'She's putting on the condition.' These are most usually said to a person's face, but it probably would not be advisable to repeat the following in a person's hearing: 'He's as heavy as a stall-fed bullock.'

The character trait of being mean or tight-fisted has yielded a rich harvest of expressions:

> She wouldn't give you the itch/the steam off her piss/the mange.
>
> She'd take the colour out of your tea.
>
> She'd mind mice at crossroads for you.
>
> He'd live in your ear.
>
> He'd take the eye out of your head and come back for the pupil.
>
> He'd take the two eyes out of your head and swear you were born blind.
>
> He'd take the salt out of the holy water.
>
> If he was in charge of daylight, we'd be in darkness half our lives.
>
> He's as tight as a duck's arse.

If someone enquired, 'Did he kill well?' after a man died, they wanted to know if there were many barrels of porter at his wake.

Some sayings involve the names of people and places, the identity of which is no longer known: 'As wrong as Moll Bell' or

'the life of Reilly'. A man who is given to flirting or reluctant to
commit to any one woman is said to have 'a rag in every bush'.
A neat dancer can 'dance inside a saucer' or 'turn on a sixpence'.

Images from nature and agriculture are plentiful, especially
describing personality traits – in particular negative ones:

He's as awkward as a spring harrow.

He's as thick as a double ditch.

Nearly never bulled the cow.

They're like a brace of briars. (People who are close-knit.)

He's as crooked as a dog's hind leg.

You could be talking to him until the cows come home and it would
do no good.

The curse of the crows. (People who are always arguing.)

She's low to the ground like a Dexter cow. (A person who is short in
stature, as is this breed of cow.)

As cracked as the crows.

I have no more a home than the hare. (The hare makes a nest or lair
in the grass rather than digging a burrow.)

He's carrying it to the fair. (Behaving in an extreme manner.)

He's as tough as *táthfhéileann*. (As tough as woodbine, the fragrant
wild flower that clings to briars and trees and is very difficult to
break.)

A head of cabbage is no good until it turns white. (This is a version of 'Age is honourable'.)

A woman from Ballinskelligs alerted me to an exclamation, 'In the name of Crom', which I had not heard around Killarney. The English equivalent is 'By Jove'. As usual, when an expression confounded me, I turned to Canon Pádraig Ó Fiannachta, who gave me the following explanation:

> Crom is the name of a malignant god, best known in the Dingle Peninsula as Crom Dubh. An ancient stone head in the wall of the old Cloghane church was regarded as his, but it was stolen about fifty or so years ago. Crom Dubh, defeated by St Brendan, was the God of Darkness, and Lúnasa was his festival too. The last Sunday in July became the traditional pilgrimage day. 'In ainm Croim' or 'By Crom' I have never heard from native speakers, but from visiting *Gaeilgeoirí*.

The broad spectrum of conditions of the mind ranging from being silly or foolish right across to being mentally unwell is covered by a variety of phrases including 'cracked', 'half cracked', 'away with the fairies', 'not the full shilling' and 'red mad'. But the kindest of phrases for a person with an intellectual disability is *duine le dia* or 'a person with God'.

Someone who overindulges in alcohol would 'drink drop-down' or 'drink Lough Erin dry'. And in the case of someone who is drinking to the point of damaging their health, he is 'shaping up for the timber overcoat'. I once heard a heavy drinker referred to as 'Tim the Thirst', and someone on a heavy drinking session is said to be 'on the ran tan' or 'on the batter'.

Cantankerous or short-tempered people are accorded their own colourful metaphors:

He'd ate (eat) you without salt.

She's a right thorny wire.

She was like a briar.

I wouldn't stand on her corns.

Exasperated or negative reactions are expressed by saying, for instance, 'The Devil mend it' or 'Bad cess to it'. Pity can be expressed by saying 'the poor devil'. When someone settles for second-best or makes a choice as a last resort, a seasonal image is invoked: 'When all fruit fails, welcome the haw.'

An elderly woman I used to know claimed to predict weather changes by the state of her feet, for instance, 'my bunions are lepping'. If her bunions were throbbing with pain, she knew rain was on the way.

One favourite expression of mine, *dríodar an chruiscín*, is generally used without translation. It means 'the drainings of the jug' and refers to a couple who have largely raised their family but who go on to have a new baby after an interval. To bring in a gwaul of hay or turf meant to carry the full of two arms of anything: derived from the Irish *gabháil*.

Leaving expressions and phrases behind and turning to individual Hiberno-English and Irish words, I will open with a childhood favourite 'mar-ee-ah', which we used to signify anything related to pretence or make-believe. It was such a normal part of speech that we had no idea that it was actually an Irish expression, *mar dhea*. For example, 'That fellow will pay you back the money, *mar dhea*.' The nearest English equivalent is 'If you believe that, you will believe anything.'

If the house was untidy, the adults would say everything was *trína chéile* or mixed up; the word could also refer to a person being disorganised or confused. Other Irish words with common currency when I was growing up in Kerry were *rí rá* (too much noise), *poulachán* (legacy) and *cráite* (upset, tormented).

In the springtime, there was always talk of *scaraveen an gcuach*, the harsh wind from the east. *Cuach* means cuckoo, the bird synonymous with the month of May. Most evocative of all is *meascán mearaí*, a term used by people to describe being overtaken by a sensation of strangeness in a field or on a mountain slope which should be familiar. *Meascán* means 'mixture' and *mearaí* is derived from *mear* or 'fast'.

The banshee was a figure from the eerie stories told in relation to death and premonitions of a death in the family; some families were said to have always heard the banshee wailing or keening immediately before a relative died. The Irish word is *bean sidhe*, a fairy woman. Closely related to the banshee was the pooka or *púca*, a mischievous fairy not unlike Shakespeare's Puck.

Another much used Irish word is *pisán*, referring to a sickly or undersized person. The diminutive version, *pisánín*, describes someone smaller again. A miserable or unfortunate person can be described as an *ainniseoir*. I have heard it used to describe a child who is whingeing. In a similar vein, a child who is not thriving can be described as *ainnis*.

If you offer some older people a drink of alcohol today, they will reply, 'I'll have a *tosheen*', which refers to *tomhaisín* or a small measure. Equally, a person who tells you they took a 'slug' of lemonade may not realise that they have just used a word derived from the Irish, *slog*, meaning to swallow by drinking.

A left-handed person is automatically called a *ciotóg*. The word, *meas*, meaning respect or approval, is one of the words which has crossed over from the Irish without corruption. For instance, 'He has no *meas* on any of his toys except that old teddy bear.' The word *grá* or love has slipped easily into the Kerry dialect also. For instance, 'I think he still has an old *grá* for her.' Terms of endearment include *a ghrá*, *a stór*, meaning treasure, and, lastly, *a chroí*, coming from the Irish for heart.

If we were whining or complaining as children, we were told to 'stop *cnámhshawling*'. This word originates from *cnáimhseáilaí*, a person who is complaining or giving out. Another admonition from childhood was to 'stop ootamawling', which meant to stop fidgeting or fumbling and originated from the Irish verb *útamáil*. A similar word was 'foostering', which comes from the word *fústar*. We were also warned that if we were not good, the 'boodie-man' would come and take us. 'Boody' is a Hiberno-English word meaning louse. In the context of 'boody-man', it could possibly mean a dirty stranger.

'Pishogue', or *piseog*, translates as a charm or spell which can be used for good or, alternately, as a kind of witchcraft to bring bad luck to a neighbour's cows or farm produce. It can also refer to superstition, for instance when some belief is dismissed by saying, 'That's only old *pishogues*.'

If a person is *leadránach*, they are long-winded or boring.

In the same vein, if you hear someone say, 'He gave the whole night *blatherawling*', you can take it that he was talking without substance or that he was full of hot air. *Blethering* is another version. *Blether* is derived from 'bladder'; in the past, animals' bladders were inflated with air to make footballs.

Then, you have *plámás* or the *plámáser*. *Plámás* means false flattery or praise.

A lanky, lazy man is called a *fostúic*. For example, 'He was a big auld foshtook of a fella.' The Irish word for bad luck, *mí-adh*, has been transplanted directly into English speech, though many might not realise the origins of the word they use like this: 'Whatever mee-aw was on him, he crashed the car a second time.' The word *teaspach*, meaning energy or high spirits, is another Irish 'loan' that has slipped seamlessly into the Kerry dialect, for example, 'That young fellow is so full of *teaspach*, he is like a spring calf that was just left out in the field.' Similarly, *gaisce* meaning great work or valour (but sometimes being boastful) is used a lot. For instance, 'He has done great *gaisce* since he took over that job.'

One of my favourite words is *praiseach* meaning 'destruction'. For instance, 'I took my eye off the pot, and the potatoes are in *praiseach*'. I once interviewed a newly appointed Kerry bishop who saw me out saying, 'Don't make *praiseach* of that now.'

Terms of endearment for children are often expressed in Irish. For example, *boyeen bán*, 'white-haired little boy' and 'a great *garsún*' (boy).

If someone or something is considered useless, the term used is *glugar*, which refers to an egg that did not hatch. Fire kindling is called *cipins*, which comes from *cipíní*, meaning little sticks. The greatest arsenal of all seems to have been reserved for people who were regarded as stupid or lacking common sense: *lúdramán, amadán, gligín, craicáilí, bostún, oinseach, dullamú* and *badarálaí*. 'Gliggeen' or 'gligín' is derived from the Irish word for a little bell, *gluigín*, and means someone who is speaking in a silly manner or tinkling.

I once heard someone describe a child-like elderly woman, who may have had some mental disability, as an *oinsín*. This was said in a kindly, compassionate spirit, but the word can mean a giddy woman. When I heard an elderly man once refer to someone as a 'right gazebo', I thought he was mixing up garden furniture, but the word translates as a 'tall awkward person'. Another pejorative description is 'boolimskee', which refers to a troublesome or boastful man. *Buailim sciath* translates as 'I strike the shield.'

Smithereens or little pieces comes from the Irish word, *smidiríni*. Sometimes I will empty a purse of loose coins on a counter and ask the shop assistant to take the 'brus' which is a derivative of *bruscar*, meaning rubbish.

Kerry people who grew up in the early decades of the twentieth century, my Gap of Dunloe grandmother included, used a lot of exclamations in Irish, many of them having reference to the world of the spirits. Some of the most common exclamations were 'wisha' taken from the Irish *mhuise* which in turn is derived from *a Mhuire*, referring to Mary, the Mother of God. For instance, 'Wisha, I could be a lot better than I am.' A fuller form of this exclamation would be *A Mhuire na bhFlaitheas* or 'O Mary of Heaven'. A very common exclamation was *Mo léir*, meaning alas, or *Mo léir chráite*. *Cráite* means tormented and the phrase could translate as 'alas and alack'. Others included *Hanam an diabhal*, which in its full form is *Th'anam don diabhal* or 'Your soul to the Devil.'

The Kerry dialect also boasts some wonderful archaic words which do not have an Irish root but nonetheless are worth remarking on. For instance, someone who would attempt a challenging physical task despite their age could be described as 'gallant'. A mischief-maker or rascal is a 'latchico' (maybe this was handed down from our Spanish forebears). Someone who does something funny or outrageous is described as 'galace'. When people in South Kerry get a notion to do something, they get a 'varie'. This is one word that has bested me as regards its origins. My hunch is that it is a derivative of 'vagary'.

Mythological references are another day's work, but I will finish with a warning given to children in the Black Valley: 'Go to bed or *Cráin* might come and get you.' *Cráin* is the Irish for a sow, an animal with many mythological associations. But of course it was all *mar dhea*.

Hidden Dingle

Up and down sloping Green Street in summertime Dingle, conversations in Spanish drift through open doors and windows. The Mediterranean timbre of the voices echoes that of Spanish merchants making their way up the hill from the wooden pier where their boats are tied up. This is Dingle in the 1500s. The merchants have been lured to the harbour town by lucrative trading opportunities, in fish and in wine. The prosperity of the times is stamped on Green Street, a Spanish quarter where the traders built their houses, often embellished with stone balconies and marble door frames.

Dingle translates as *An Daingean* or *Daingean Uí Chúi*s, meaning the stronghold of Ó Chúis, a Gaelic chieftain who ruled the area prior to the Norman invasion of 1169. There is a reference to the chieftain in the *Annals of the Four Masters* which were compiled by Franciscan friars in the 1600s.

Commerce with Spain and France in the sixteenth century made the West Kerry harbour town the second most important port on the Irish west coast after Galway. In an expression of devotion to their patron saint, St James, the wealthy Spaniards built their own church on Main Street and dedicated it to him. The harbour was a popular starting point for the medieval pilgrimage to Santiago de Compostella. Foreign influence was commonplace. A survey taken of harbours along the coast in this era rounds off most entries with the observation, 'Many people speak Spanish here.' People had a smattering of the language right through the Dingle Peninsula across to the Blasket Islands.

The two best-known landmarks in Green Street today are the Catholic parish church of St Mary's and, directly across from it, Dick Mack's Bar. It is here that I begin my exploration of the town with Bernard Goggin, naturalist, former publisher and a walking encyclopaedia on West Kerry. At the top of the street, there is a large two-storey corner house, Rice House, in which rooms were once prepared by the Rice family to accommodate Marie Antoinette of France. Count James Louis Rice hatched a plan to rescue the imprisoned queen, who is said to have chosen her husband and children over liberty. (Bernard tells me that Count Rice was the inspiration for the character Barry Lyndon of the novel and film of the same name.) The house was once a presbytery, and the back yard was known as the 'Canon's Garden'.

Across from Rice House in Green Street, the upper storey of the third house down has the year 1586 set between decorative stones, and a few doors down, a Spanish motif of two birds, also set in a façade, once signified a bordello. Not all the services that sprang up on the affluent coat-tails of the influx of foreigner merchants were licit.

Beside St Mary's church, a decorative iron gateway leads into the cultural and spiritual centre, An Díseart, developed by retired university professor, author and former Dingle parish priest, Monsignor Pádraig Ó Fiannachta, whose many scholarly feats include editing and translating the Bible into Irish in 1982. Among the treasures in the former Presentation convent building is an upstairs chapel featuring masterpieces by the stained-glass artist Harry Clarke, created in 1922 at the peak of his career. Six twin-lighted lancet windows depict key events in the life of Christ. Twin-lighted windows are a feature of Gothic architecture where a slender stone division separates the two halves of one large window. The chapel roof and walls are made of Spanish oak and the altar of Italian marble. A fresco and a series of murals feature in other rooms. The An Díseart garden is a peaceful oasis and is open to the public.

About three doors below the church is a house which is thought to have belonged to the original Spanish settlement. Over the door is an image of an eagle grasping a smaller bird in its talons. Bernard believes the eagle image to be Galician. Three of the original Spanish houses were still intact when he was growing up in the 1950s. He recalled one of the street's shopkeepers, Katie Sarah, who had another life in Chicago before she ended up back in Dingle selling bulls-eyes across her shop counter. Jostled by a stranger one day in the American city, she is reputed to have said, 'Watch where you're going big fella.' The stranger turned out to be the mobster Al Capone, who replied, 'God, I love the Irish.'

Halfway down Green Street we turn left into Grey's Lane, which took its name from a local solicitor in the early nineteenth century. The big house on the corner was once the home of Captain de Moleyn, who was Lord Ventry's brother and his land agent at the end of the nineteenth century and into the beginning of the twentieth. It later functioned as a branch of the Munster and Leinster Bank and is now a private house. Set into the stone wall running the length of the laneway behind the house are the remains of a small slated building which served as the estate office of Lord Ventry, who, Bernard explains, once owned 90,000 acres in West Kerry. Bricked-up archways indicate stables and coach houses inside the wall.

At the end of Grey's Lane, a left turn leads into Dingle Town Park, a large green area spreading out in a direct line from the steeple of St Mary's and behind the houses and yards of Green Street. Dingle was a walled town when it was a preserve of the earls of Desmond. Bernard has been told by archaeologists that remnants of the original structure still endure in parts of the back wall of the park. There were references to the wall right through the sixteenth century, one in relation to money given by Queen Elizabeth I for its repair. The parts that still exist are a registered national monument, according to Bernard, who added that the money collected for their construction was called 'murage'. This area has been known as 'the Orchard' for years, but Bernard suggests that the name is a corruption of 'Archard', a term used since the thirteenth century to describe a firing range for longbows. His theory is that people interpreted it as 'orchard' in the twentieth century.

After the Town Park, Grey's Lane meets Dykegate Lane, which is pronounced 'Dagget Lane' by locals. In 1607 King James granted Dingle a charter which had been sanctioned by Queen Elizabeth in 1585. This led to Dingle becoming a walled town, the gates of which were located in Dykegate Lane which is divided from the next street, The Mall, by the eponymous river. There are buildings on either side of the Mall today, but the area was still largely a marsh in the 1840s, and the road through it was built quite late in the development of the town. At one end of it was the three-storey Royal Irish Constabulary (RIC) barracks; the garda station now stands on the site.

From the end of the Mall over to the section of the town at the end of Green Street stretched the Holy Ground, so-called because of the holes in the surface rather than any claim to sanctity. There was a big leather export trade to Spain, and part of the tanning process involved soaking the leather in the holes in the ground. 'The holes were filled with human urine which was freely given by the townspeople,' Bernard said.

In the direction of the town centre, a stone with a cross inscribed in the centre is set into the perimeter wall of Russell's Guesthouse; the stone marks the location of St John's Well, which has been covered over. This was a holy well, pictures of which may be seen in current photographic books of Dingle. Further along this row, the houses are prime examples of the use of old red sandstone, a common building material in Dingle. The town's former Protestant school is in this row as is the Christian Brothers parochial school, which dates back to 1846. Bernard explains that the Christian Brothers came to Dingle in the 1840s to counter a Protestant evangelical drive to convert Catholics through the peninsula and out on the Blaskets.

The former bridewell on the Mall was used for storing salt when its time for holding prisoners had passed, recalled Bernard, adding that mackerel were still being salted in Dingle in the early 1950s.

At the Dingle Courthouse, there are windblown patterns in the finer sandstone which was used in the cornerstones of buildings, as well as a plaque in memory of John Francis Marshall Milos, MD, JP, who was Medical Officer for Dingle for forty-two years and who died on 16 May 1912. Bernard's great-grandmother, a Neligan from Lough Farm on the eastern edge of the town, worked as a herbalist for him.

Beyond the Mall is Bridge House, which was the base for Irish soldiers during the Second World War; a sentry with fixed bayonet stood outside it. Bridge House stands at the start of John Street, which was the old entrance to Dingle. Just off John Street is the sportsfield, at the edge of which was located a Norman ring fort built to guard the settlement – by 1200 Dingle was heavily Normanised.

At the higher end of John Street there was a hangman's stone, where corpses were left on display as a deterrent to anyone entering the town. On the town side of John Street is the Small Bridge or *An Droichead Bheag* on which the Dingle Pipe Band gathers on New Year's Eve. Downriver is the Spa Road in the vicinity of which there used to be a brewery and the fair field. Carpenters used the river water to cool metal bands for the wheels of horse cars here.

The 1830s saw a new wave of prosperity in Dingle and the rebuilding of Main Street to accommodate merchants' houses, sweeping away any remnants of the three Norman castles on the street. The Castle of the Ravens stood at the top right-hand side of Main Street behind the Temperance Hall, a second castle stood behind Fitzgeralds' shop and a third behind the AIB building.

Halfway up Main Street on the right is St James's Church of Ireland church, which replaced the earlier Catholic church of St James built by the Spanish community. It became a Protestant church after the Reformation. Care must be taken walking on the rough ground of the graveyard, but, exploring it, the centuries roll away. One of the most striking finds for me was a horizontal headstone of the Desmonds, decorated with the family emblems of a boar and a dragon-like griffin. There is also a Mullins family grave which dates back to 1695. According to Bernard, the Mullins' lineage can be traced back to a Cromwellian army officer who was granted a large tract of land in the area. After Sir Thomas Mullins acquired the title

Lord Ventry in 1800, the name Mullins was changed to de Moleyn, which was a throw-back to the family's Norman roots.

Ancient carved stones from the original Spanish church, including a dripstone, are scattered here and there. (A dripstone is an architectural feature on a door or a window for handling rainwater.) One of the oldest grave slabs dates back to 1504 and may have been mounted on the wall of the old church of Saint James's originally.

Bernard's and my walk brought us full circle and back to Rice House, outside which the Day of the Killing of the Men, or *Lá Maraithe na bhFear*, took place in June 1793, when a large crowd gathered to protest about rents; fourteen protestors were killed by the English military under the command of a member of the local landed gentry. A woman is understood to have lost her life as well. There is no plaque to mark the massacre.

However, close by, the Treaty of Dingle on 28 April 1529 is commemorated. The treaty was concluded between James FitzGerald, 11th Earl of Desmond and Don Gonzalo Fernández, Ambassador Plenipotentiary of the Holy Roman Emperor of the German Nation and King of Spain, Charles V. The information plaque on the treaty uses the original spelling of Hapsburg, 'Habsburg'. This treaty gave a formal legal and constitutional foundation to the rights of citizenship and other privileges that Irish exiles and émigrés enjoyed in Hapsburg Spain, Hapsburg Austria and Hapsburg Netherlands (present-day Belgium and Luxembourg) from the sixteenth to the early twentieth centuries. 'As a result of the treaty, a "Dingler" could go to Vienna and Peru, trade and be protected as an equal citizen of the Hapsburg empire,' Bernard said. 'It remained in force until

1952. After the First World War, the empire had disintegrated. The Bishops of Ireland, the original control freaks, closed down the treaty because they did not want clergy, who they had not taught, coming into Ireland from overseas. They got on to De Valera, who got on to Franco. Franco had to bring in a law to end the Irish rights and privileges.'

We head down Green Street again and turn right into The Strand, a street that opens out onto the pier and the waterfront. Another right-hand turn leads into a narrow street lined on the left with little cottages which have survived from the Lower Colony, set out in 1830 for converts to Protestantism. The Upper Colony in John Street has since been demolished. Bernard describes the Colony as the original 'gated condominium', with walls running on the other side of it. He remembers women chatting to each other over the half doors which were designed to keep children in and geese and ganders out.

Close to the Colony was the home of the late Maurice Griffin, founder of *The Kerryman* newspaper, and the former home of the Goggin family, which also served as the local telephone exchange, employing sixteen operators. Across the street is 'The Tracks', where the railway ran right out to the pier. The railway station, which was located closer to the town, still stands and is used as a funeral parlour today – the final destination, but for a different realm.

Ventry's U-boat

Ventry Harbour on the Dingle Peninsula was the setting for one of the most remarkable expressions of humanitarian spirit during the Second World War, when a German U-boat surfaced in the bay on 4 October 1939 and deposited twenty-eight Greek sailors on the shore in sight of an astonished audience of locals.

A Greek freighter, the *Diamantis*, had been torpedoed by U-35 the previous day, and the German captain had taken the crew on board before the attack. News of the unexpected visitors took wings that foggy Wednesday afternoon in *Ceann Trá*, the Head of the Strand, and its surrounds, prompting adults and children to rush to *Rinn Stiabhana* where the submarine had surfaced from waters more usually traversed by black canoes and fishing trawlers.

Among the onlookers who gathered to watch the drama unfold some time after 4 p.m. was eleven-year-old Jimmy Fenton of Ballymore, who had just come home from school. In 1984 Fenton, since deceased, recalled that he had run a quarter of a mile to see the submarine. Another schoolboy, Bearnard Ó Lubhaing, whose family ran the village post office in Ventry, described the strange sight years later in the memoir he wrote as a retired teacher. He related that the submarine was anchored only twenty yards from the rocks and that the crew of the *Diamantis* were put ashore in a rubber dinghy. As postmaster,

Bearnard's father had access to one of the few telephones in the area; he rang the garda superintendent in Dingle to alert him to the strange happenings at the ocean's edge.

The Greek crew members were put ashore 'in full view of the whole countryside' in the space of about an hour and were taken into the farmhouse of the Cleary family. Before the gardaí arrived on the scene, U-35 had cruised out a couple of hundred yards from the coast and submerged beneath the waves. Empty cigarette boxes and chocolate wrappers left behind by the Greeks were gathered by the local children as souvenirs of the landing.

The story went round that the submarine captain had informed the sailors that a Dingle publican, Michael Long, would take care of them and that they were to have a pint at the quayside bar and remember him to the owner; it was said he had visited Long's bar before the war. As it was to transpire, this embellishment was an example of the truth not being allowed to get in the way of a good story. When former U-boat captain Werner F. R. Lott, then aged seventy-seven, visited West Kerry in September 1984, he told *Kerryman* journalist Marese McDonagh that it was, in fact, his first time setting foot on Irish soil.

On that visit he spent most of his time in Castlegregory, on the coast between Tralee and Dingle. He also toured the Ring of Kerry and took a jaunting car trip in Killarney. He met Jimmy Fenton at the site of the landing and posed for pictures with him. He also visited the hospital, where a plaque had been erected to the sailors and, it is said, actually sank a few pints in Michael Long's bar. Jimmy conveyed to Lott how grateful the

Greeks had been to him for saving their lives. 'Their English was bad but they kept saying, "German gut man",' Jimmy recalled.

The former U-35 captain said he remembered every detail surrounding the event. His decision resulted in a severe reprimand from the Third Reich government for breaching Irish neutrality to save the lives of the twenty-eight seamen. 'I had stopped a Greek ship in the waters round Land's End,' Lott said. 'Under the Geneva Convention, I could stop it and, if it was carrying provisions for the enemy, I could destroy it.' He said that, in the rough weather, he had not been able to examine the ship's papers, so a signal was given to follow him to Irish waters where the weather would be less rough. When the ship failed to follow him, he fired a shot at its bow, resulting in the crew panicking and jumping into the lifeboats, which overturned. 'It is almost unbelievable but we picked them all up,' he remembered.

The *Diamantis* had been carrying 4,000 tons of iron ore when it was sunk off Land's End. Captain Lott had twenty-eight Greeks and twenty-three Germans on board and limited provisions. He decided to leave his extra passengers off in Ventry and remembered anchoring seven yards off the shore. He described the manoeuvre to Marese McDonagh:

> We had one little boat and one of my men rowed the Greeks two at a time ashore. He made the trip fourteen times and a crowd gathered to watch. When the Greek sailors said goodbye to me on the conning tower, they went on their knees and kissed my wedding ring as if I was a bishop. I did not want this but they said, 'We owe our lives to you, you have treated us very nicely.'

As regards the severe reprimand he received for his actions, the captain said it had been clear to him that he was breaching Irish neutrality but that he had done so 'for humanity's sake'. 'I thought this would be understood,' he said. 'Of course the Irish government protested to the German government and I got a severe reprimand. Of course this clearly was justified.'

Two months after his Ventry 'visit', Lott's submarine was sunk off the coast of Norway by a fleet commanded by Lord Louis Mountbatten. The two 'foes' were to develop a lifelong friendship. When he thanked the British commander for saving them from the freezing waters – after forty-five minutes in the water his hands were so numb he could not grip the rope – Mountbatten replied, 'That is how life is. You were extraordinary picking up the Greeks.'

Werner Lott, who had been reared in an East African colony where his father was a doctor, went on to spend most of the war in captivity, initially in the Tower of London and later in Canada, where he spent time on the east coast before being transferred to a log cabin in the Rockies. When Marese McDonagh commented on his command of English, he replied with a smile, 'I spent so many years behind barbed wire I had plenty of time to learn.'

On his second night of imprisonment in his 'medieval cell' in the Tower of London, Lott went on hunger strike; because of his rank he objected strongly to the dire conditions. Mountbatten responded by arranging for the Admiralty to allow Lott and his second-in-command to dine at Scott's Restaurant on the condition they would not try to escape. They were returned to their cells after the taste of London nightlife.

In October 2009 Ventry Historical Society hosted a special commemoration on the occasion of the seventieth anniversary of the landing. The German Ambassador, Dr Busso von Alvensleben, unveiled a memorial in the green area in the centre of Ventry. The unprepossessing inscribed stone bears witness to one of the most dramatic events ever to unfold in the peaceful harbour.

On the Edge

Mystery surrounds the origins of a tiny stone doll found during excavations at the monastic site at Riasc on the Dingle Peninsula; the thoughts and emotions of the person in whose hands the carved image took shape have left no impression on the sands of time. Possibly the painstaking task was a translation of grief into a labour of love, a mind-numbing distraction from the pain of loss. The doll was found in the *cillín*, an area reserved for unbaptised children in the post-medieval section of the graveyard. The term *cillín*, small church, refers to a children's burial ground, the plural of which is *cillínigh*. Other versions are *ceallúnaigh*, *caldragh* and *callúragh*. The *cillín* was identified as a 'Callúragh Burial Ground' on the Ordnance Survey maps of 1841–2 and 1892–8, indicating that it was still being used for that purpose during those times. Burial grounds, such as the one at Riasc, were still being used well into the twentieth century all over the country.

The stone carving has not moved far from the place where its earthen slumber was disturbed by the archaeologists. It is now part of a collection of historical and archaeological artefacts on exhibit at *Músaem Chorca Dhuibhne* (Dingle Peninsula Museum) in the village of *Baile an Fheirtéaraigh* (Ballyferriter). It is one of several items from the Riasc site on display, which are on loan from the National Museum of Ireland. Archaeologist and museum curator Isabel Bennett said the carved piece was difficult to date precisely; she suggested it could have originated any time from the post-medieval period up to the earlier years of the twentieth century. It was associated with one of the several small, box-like graves found to the east of the site. 'I suppose it shows that the child buried – and very few if any skeletal remains survived at this site due to the acid nature of the soil – was very much wanted, so much so that the little doll was carved for it.'

According to Isabel, it is very unusual to find 'grave goods' in burials in a Christian context, but these burials would have been very much 'on the edge'. Being on the edge is a reference to the liminal or boundary locations of the majority of the *cillínigh*: a reflection of the Catholic teaching on Limbo, which regarded the souls of unbaptised babies as being suspended in a state between Heaven and Hell. (In Latin, *limbus* means edge or boundary.) While the *cillínigh* are primarily associated with babies, other burials also took place there, for instance, bodies of those who took their own lives or unidentified bodies washed up by the sea.

The *cillínigh* are mostly found on private land in Kerry: on shingles, in ring forts, on cliff edges, in abandoned church sites, near roads or paths, outside graveyards, neither here nor there. They were used to a limited degree right up to the 1960s. One burial ground near the ruins of Ardea Castle, in the parish of Tuosist outside Kenmare, is virtually part of the front garden of a bungalow. The small stones, set close to the ground, are unmarked, apart from one dated 1766. There are about thirteen *cillínigh* scattered throughout Tuosist. The infants were usually buried at twilight or before dawn by the men of the family with neither the mother nor any other women present. They were buried in unconsecrated ground because it was considered that original sin had not been 'washed' from their souls by the waters of baptism. Sometimes a mother would not even know where her baby was buried.

According to archaeologist Emer A. Dennehy from Tralee, the realm of Limbo for infants in Irish society was colloquially referred to as *dorchadas gan phian*, darkness without pain, 'for although these children would forever be denied the light of the face of God, they had committed no actual crime and unlike others in Limbo they would suffer no pain'. Some of the key findings of her Master's study on the history of the *ceallúnaigh* in Kerry have been presented in the *Kerry Archaeological and Historical Society Journal*. Dennehy placed the introduction of these specific burial grounds in the context of the debate concerning the interpretation of original sin and its implication on the afterlife of the unbaptised. It culminated in the 'denial of burial rites to these unbaptised infants, and resulted in the establishment of alternate burial grounds, hidden from public view and public shame'. The journal article relates that one of the most predominant themes in Irish folklore regarding unbaptised infants was their haunting of people, priests in particular, until such time as they would be baptised and named, allowing them to rest in peace.

Dennehy also lists some unusual traditions surviving in folklore on the burial of infants. 'One such tradition states that no stones should be placed at the foot of a child's grave; this is to enable it to continue to grow in the afterlife. Another tradition recommends that the body of an illegitimate child should be buried face-downwards. This is to ensure that the man who fathered the child would become infertile. One remaining tradition is the belief that vessels should be placed with the graves, to allow the infants to drink milk in the afterlife.' She explains that the shame and fear of the unknown were reflected not only in the isolation of the burial grounds from communal areas but also through their location near physical boundaries, reflecting the marginal nature of those interred. 'Ceallúnaigh are an important part of Irish and European history, and they should not be forgotten,' she concluded.

Rescuing Marie Antoinette

It sounds like the stuff of fiction: a daring plot hatched in Dingle to rescue Marie Antoinette from her prison in the heart of Revolutionary Paris and smuggle her to Kerry via

Nantes in a wine merchant's ship. Strange as it may sound in the telling, there is documentary evidence to substantiate the existence of this escape plan, which has been part of Dingle folklore for years.

Local myths include that of a secret tunnel from the harbour to a town-centre house, Rice House, which had been prepared as a temporary hideaway for the Queen of France. The rescue attempt was planned between August 1792 and January 1793 while Austrian-born Marie Antoinette and King Louis XVI were closely guarded in the Temple, a medieval fortress in Paris. Austria was key to the Dingle connection with the ill-fated queen in an era when there were strong economic and religious ties between Ireland and the Continent. Beleaguered by their Protestant foes in England, the Catholic Irish ascendancy turned time and again to the monarchies of France, Spain, Italy and Austria for assistance.

Into this scenario steps James Louis Rice, a descendant of a Norman Welsh family, originally called Rhys, who settled in Dingle in the late 1100s. The Rice family home was in Burnham, or *Baile an Ghoilín*, across the harbour from Dingle, where the Irish-speaking secondary school, Coláiste Íde, is now located. Born in 1730, James Louis was a son of Thomas Rice, alias 'Black Tom', a Dingle wine merchant who profited handsomely from trade with France and Spain.

Like many wealthy Catholic families denied educational opportunities under the Penal Laws, a discriminatory body of legislation introduced in the 1600s, the Rices sent James Louis abroad to be educated. After a spell studying for the priesthood at a Franciscan seminary in Leuven, Belgium, he joined the Irish

Brigade in Austria, rising quickly through the ranks. The late Canon John McKenna, writing about the Dingle connection to the French Revolution, said that James Louis became an 'intimate friend' of the Austrian Emperor, Joseph II, whom he had met when they were both students at the military academy. 'The Emperor conferred on him and his father, Tom Rice, the title of Count of the Holy Roman Empire.' The Emperor had a younger sister, who, at the age of fifteen, married a Frenchman, Louis, who acceded to the French throne in 1774: King Louis XVI. It is entirely plausible that James Louis Rice, mixing in court circles in Vienna, had known Marie Antoinette.

Pat Neligan, a local historian in Dingle, fills out the picture of the well-connected young military officer with access to the highest levels of society in Austria due to his connection with the Emperor. 'He was a frequent guest at the soirees and the official balls at the Schönbrunn Palace, the impressive imperial home on the outskirts of Vienna.' James Louis' friendship with the Austrian royals, his years of military experience and his family's shipping network all combined to make him an ideal candidate to mastermind an escape bid.

He enlisted the help of Thomas Trant, a Ventry man serving with the Irish Brigade in France, William Hickie from Ballylongford in North Kerry and a Count Waters of Paris, who was married to James Louis' sister, Mary Rice, and whose ancestors came from Macroom, County Cork. The plan was to bribe the prison guards and, using relays of horses, to get Marie Antoinette swiftly to the coast, where a wine ship would be waiting to bring her to Dingle. She was to be accommodated in Rice House until she could be brought to London and from there conveyed safely to Vienna. At the time, her husband was confined in separate quarters because of an earlier ill-fated escape bid, the 'Flight to Varennes', which complicated the plan of James Louis and his cohorts. 'The plan failed because Marie Antoinette would not leave Paris without the King, even though it was impossible for the rescue group to include him in the escape bid,' according to Canon McKenna.

Marie Antoinette was beheaded on 16 October 1793.

The story represents one of the great 'what ifs' of history and is also a powerful demonstration of the sophisticated European alliances forged by Kerry people centuries before the concept of the European Union was even dreamt of. In June 2010 the Austrian Ambassador to Ireland, Dr Walter Hagg, unveiled a plaque at Rice House to commemorate the link with Marie Antoinette. 'The people of Ireland, Kerry and Dingle can be proud of having had such courageous and brave people,' Dr Hagg said. The Ambassador also spoke about the fact that James Louis Rice was one of more than 2,500 Irish officers who served in the Hapsburg Imperial Army between 1620 and 1918. He said there were other links between Kerry and Austria that went back to the Middle Ages. 'In Vienna we had the Irish Abbey in the centre of the city which dated from 1165 and was run exclusively by Irish monks from Kerry – no Austrians were admitted!'

Finding Nimmo

For a man with such an influential role in developing strategic elements of Kerry's infrastructure in the first half of the 1800s, Alexander Nimmo (1783–1832) is little remembered in the county today. In stark contrast to the modern practice of naming roads, bridges and even roundabouts after various personages (often politicians), the name of the pioneering Scottish engineer has all but slipped into oblivion in Kerry, apart from some references in academic journals. A bridge outside Cahersiveen was named after him but it has since been bypassed. The considerable legacy of Nimmo, who lived in Ireland from 1811 to 1832, endures, however, in stretches of the world-famous Ring of Kerry coastal route. The road from Kenmare to Glengarriff, where the remarkable tunnels are an engineering feat in themselves, is also the work of the civil engineer.

Nimmo was born in Cupar, Fife, in 1783. As well as being a watchmaker, his father ran a hardware store in Kirkcaldy. Educated at the University of Saint Andrews from 1796 to 1799, and at the University of Edinburgh for a year, Nimmo was an accomplished scholar in Latin, Greek, logic, ethics and natural philosophy. He also distinguished himself in algebra and the higher branches of mathematics.

While he was working as a headmaster at the Academy of Inverness, Nimmo carried out some survey work for the engineer Thomas Telford, who, in 1811, recommended him for a position with the Bog Commission of Ireland. His teaching days were over from then on. Nimmo's work was part of a drive begun by the British government in 1809 to assess the potential of Ireland's bogs to be converted into agricultural land to absorb some of Ireland's fast-growing population. This was done in the general context of trying to maximise Ireland's natural resources at the time.

Nimmo was aged twenty-nine when he arrived in Kerry with a brief to assess the 'practicability of draining and cultivating the bogs'. He went on to make a monumental contribution to the economic and social life of the Iveragh Peninsula, which had been significantly isolated because of poor to nonexistent road access. He surveyed the bogs of the peninsula and carried out a comprehensive assessment of the economy of the Iveragh Peninsula for the British government.

Dr Arnold Horner, a retired University College Dublin geography professor, has written a commentary on the map and report which Nimmo prepared. He notes that the map showed Iveragh thirty years before the decade of the Great Famine and half a century before it became a crucial location for transatlantic communication, observing as follows:

> Here is Iveragh long before the advent of the pioneer tourists, at a time when it was still quite isolated from the rest of Ireland. Towns and villages – Cahirciveen, Waterville, Portmagee – were still in their infancy. The only landward access for carriages was the difficult 'butter road' that rose to nearly 1,000 feet over sea level on the flanks of Drung Hill; most of the present Ring of Kerry route had yet to be constructed.

In his 1812 report Nimmo observed that though the harbour of Valentia was well adapted to the reception of ships of all descriptions, the effect it had on agriculture could be guessed by 'the bog growing down to the water's edge ... Destitute therefore of a market, of roads and wheel-carriages, this barony seems to have little temptation to increase its corn culture.' He exclaimed at the fact that in the whole peninsula of about 400 square miles, 'no such thing as a plough is known'. The spade in use, he noted, was not a common garden spade but an implement with an iron blade about five inches broad. Also, hardly a tree was to be seen in the barony because the original woods were destroyed by 'iron forges, near a century ago'.

The only carriage road into Iveragh wound around the steep slope of Drung Hill between Cahersiveen and Kells 'at an elevation of 800 feet'. Nimmo wrote that the road was so 'ill-adapted to wheel carriages that there is hardly an implement of that kind in the whole barony'. Butter, the chief produce of the county, was carried entirely on horseback over Drung, each horse bearing two or three firkins weighing between 1 and 1.5 hundredweight, to the Cork Butter Market almost 80 miles away. Nimmo's solution was to develop a new Drung Road along the lower part of the hill between Mountain Stage and Kells, just beyond the seaside village of Glenbeigh. The road, which connected Drung with the 'low country of Kerry', was completed in 1824; it was the foundation of this scenic stretch of the Ring of Kerry route, as it is known today.

Writing on 1 March 1824, Nimmo was buoyant in tone as he finished his report with this commentary on the changes wrought by the new road:

I cannot conclude this report without alluding to the rapid improvement which is taking place in the barony of Iveragh since the construction of this Road.

A few years ago there was hardly a plough, car, or carriage of any kind; the butter the only produce, as carried to Cork on horseback; there was not a decent public-house, and I think only one house slated and plastered in the village of Caherseveen [*sic*]; the rest a few scattered thatched cabins; the nearest post office thirty miles distant.

The transformation of Cahersiveen by the road was evident in the addition of:

... twenty respectable two-storey houses, slated and plastered with good sash windows; a respectable shop with cloth, hardware and groceries, a comfortable inn with six bedrooms and six horse stable; a post office, bridewell, new chapel; a quay which is covered with limestone; a salt work, and, perhaps, forty cars and carts, and a resident gentleman's coach.

The architect of this expansion concluded with optimism, 'I have no doubt of the continuance of the prosperity of this place, and of the consequent improvement of the whole barony.'

Outside of Kerry, Nimmo was also involved in the construction of roads and piers in the west of Ireland. Author Kathleen Villiers-Tuthill from Clifden, County Galway, in her book on Nimmo's contribution to the 'Western District', related how he referred to himself as 'an observing traveller' and how he had commented in particular on the living conditions of the poor. 'The choices he made determined which villages survived and which were abandoned, which districts were marginalised and which were developed,' she wrote.

Nimmo died at his Dublin home, 78 Marlborough Street, on the evening of 20 January 1832, at the age of forty-nine. *The Times* reported that he had been an invalid from rheumatic pains for some time and attributed his death to 'dropsy', an archaic medical term for oedema. The Scotsman had given most of his professional life to improving the social conditions in the south and the west of Ireland. His personal life, including his time in Kerry and his final years in Dublin, remain as shrouded as his creation on Drung Hill when the Atlantic mist sweeps in.

Ancient Cahersiveen

One of the best-kept secrets in Cahersiveen (*Cathair Saidhbhín*: the stone fort of Saidhbhín) lies at the end of Old Market Street, just a few minutes' walk from the O'Connell Memorial Church. Here you will find a peaceful green oasis of ancient ruins shaded by young sycamore trees tucked away behind the houses and backyards of Main Street.

When I visited in September, there were tangles of lush blackberries entwined around old tombs of natural stone topped with slabs of Valentia slate; birds provided the backing track. Retired teacher Junior Murphy revealed this tranquil corner of Cahersiveen to me and pointed out the most interesting features, including the tomb of Daniel O'Connell's parents, Morgan and Catherine. Their tomb is set on the outside of the eastern gable of the fifteenth-century Abbey of the Holy Cross, under its lancet window. The gable and the western wall are all that remain of the ancient church, believed to have been established by Augustinians from Continental Europe.

Across the way from the Abbey ruins is a Protestant church with a tower, built in 1815. Junior points out the open book or Bible motif over the church door; the square tower is still intact. Thomas Reid, author of *Travels in Ireland*, published in 1822, describes attending this church with only seven people in the congregation while close by the Catholic church only had room for a third of its congregation. He was referring to the Penal Church which still stands, not within the green area, but at the edge of the car park. It is now under private ownership. The building also acted as a school, and Daniel O'Connell may have been baptised there, Junior adds. The church served as a centre of worship until 1823, when a new church was built on a site provided by O'Connell.

From church to pub. We return to Main Street, a meeting place for the people of South Kerry and a street with links to the famous. The Anchor Bar on Main Street was once the home of the late Pauline McGuire, whose play *The Last Move* was performed in the Abbey Theatre. When I met Pauline in 1991 and mentioned the play to her, she threw her eyes to Heaven, as if she was weary of references to it. She leafed through her visitors' book for me, though, picking out names such as Mike Dukakis, former Governor of Massachusetts, and

George Bernard Shaw biographer Michael Holyroyd. And just for the record, she told me, Charlie Chaplin used to have his hair cut on Main Street by barber John McCarthy. The short-story writer Benedict Kiely penned the first draft of his 'The Dogs in the Great Glen' in Pauline McGuire's kitchen. It is a marvellous short story that made it to the curriculum of the old Intermediate Certificate. Pauline told me that Kiely drew much of his inspiration from stories told to him by her late father, Michael O'Shea.

Publican Kevin O'Connor, who ran Teach Culainn back in the days when I met Pauline, would have looked as much at home sipping espresso in Monterey, California, as serving up pints of plain in Main Street – 'and the farther up you go, the "maner" [meaner] it gets,' he quipped. Kevin recalled his childhood days for me and spoke of Dr Healy, who brought a touch of country to the street. Healy had a dairy herd behind his house, and his cows' lowing could be heard through Main Street in the mornings as they were brought down from the slopes of Beentee mountain. Kevin also told me a story about a townsman who kept his Christmas crib in the window all year round. When a local wit, Parnell, was asked if there were many animals at the fair day, he replied, 'There's more animals below in Jim Flynn's crib.'

The elderly woman of the house in one of the town's watering holes took a healthy interest in her customers. A young couple of tourists were subjected to the following gentle inquisition: 'Are ye on holidays? Are ye married? Have ye children?' When the last question met with a negative, she countered, 'Are ye trying?'

Tarbert House.
Courtesy of photographer Michael Cowhey, the Limerick Leader.

Ursula Leslie outside Tarbert House in 2013.
Courtesy of photographer Michael Cowhey, the Limerick Leader.

Gunsborough Villa, Ballylongford, possible birthplace of Lord Herbert Horatio Kitchener. *Courtesy of Rattoo Heritage Society.*

Journalist Seamus McConville (1932–2012) was editor of *The Kerryman* from 1974 until his retirement in 1988, and he continued as a contributor until shortly before his death. *Courtesy of photographer Kevin Coleman.*

Crotta Great House near Kilflynn, boyhood home of Lord Herbert Horatio Kitchener. *Courtesy of Rattoo Heritage Society.*

Mai Quillinan outside her home on Church Street, Listowel. *Courtesy of the Kerryman Archive, Kerry County Library; photographer Brendan Landy, Listowel.*

Bryan and Kitty MacMahon
at their home in Church
Street, Listowel, in 1991.
*Courtesy of the Kerryman
Archive, Kerry County
Library; photographer
Brendan Landy, Listowel.*

Cornie Tangney and his
terrier, Latchico, in the
kitchen of his home at
Mount, Scartaglin, on 6
March 1990. *Courtesy of
photographer John Reidy.*

Champion international competitors, athlete Tom McCarthy, cyclist Dan Ahern and mountain runner John Lenihan in 2013 at Glanageenty Woods, where their stellar achievements are honoured along the forest walk. *Courtesy of John Lenihan.*

The unveiling of the Pikeman Statue in Denny Street, Tralee, on 21 September 1902 by Maud Gonne. *Courtesy of Tómas Slattery, Tralee.*

Monsignor Pádraig Ó Fiannachta, Dingle, in the Díseart chapel which boasts six Harry Clarke stained glass windows. *Courtesy of photographer Valerie O'Sullivan.*

Former U-boat Commander Werner Lott with Seán Cleary, Ballymore, Ventry, in September 1984, as he revisits the area in which he landed a Greek crew in 1939.
Courtesy of the Kerryman Archive, Kerry County Library, Tralee; photographer Kevin Coleman.

The Riasc stone doll at *Músaem Chorca Dhuibhne*. An artefact from the collection of the National Museum of Ireland. *Image reproduced courtesy of the National Museum of Ireland; photographer Siobhán Dempsey.*

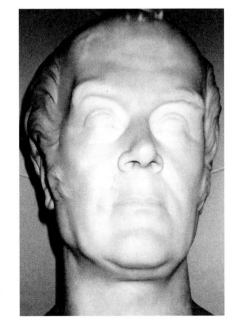

Bust of Scottish Engineer Alexander Nimmo at the RDS, Ballsbridge, Dublin. *Photo courtesy of Dr Arnold Horner.*

Junior Murphy, Cahersiveen, pictured outside the ruined Bahaghs Workhouse which had 1,241 residents at the height of the Famine in 1848. *Courtesy of photographer Alan Landers.*

Derrynane House, home of Daniel O'Connell, 'The Liberator', at Caherdaniel, *c.* 1945. *Courtesy of the Department of Arts, Heritage and the Gaeltacht.*

Mrs Kate Dore (*centre*), housekeeper for the Delap family, Valentia Island, *c.* 1930s. *Courtesy of Joanna Lee, Dublin.*

From left: Constance (Connie), Mary and Maude Delap, pictured at Reenellen House, Valentia Island, *c.* 1930s. *Courtesy of Joanna Lee, Dublin.*

The late Pádraig and Joan Kennelly, who founded the *Kerry's Eye* newspaper in 1974 and lived and worked at 22 Ashe Street, Tralee. *Courtesy of Kerry's Eye.*

Big Bertha (47) celebrates her birthday with RTÉ broadcaster Joe Duffy, owner Jerome O'Leary, publican Teddy O'Neill (*left*), and friends at the Blackwater Tavern, Sneem, on 10 March 1992.
Courtesy of photographer Kevin Coleman.

Flemish artist Lily van
Oost in the Black Valley in
the 1980s.
Courtesy of Kerry's Eye.

Killarney House, seat of the earls of Kenmare, which was located at Knockreer and was destroyed by fire in 1913. *Courtesy of the Lawrence Collection.*

RIC Barracks, Lewis Road, Killarney.
Courtesy of the Lawrence Collection.

Michael Leane, Noel Grimes and James O'Connor of Killarney
Historical Society at St Mary's Holy Well, Killarney, in 2013.
Courtesy of photographer Michael Brosnan, Currow.

Jack O'Shea (*seated centre*), with the 1938 Muckross Juvenile Six Winners. *Front*: Paddy Daly and Frank Murhill; *back*: Paddy O'Neill, Harry Price, Gerald Doyle and Patrick Mulligan. *Courtesy of John Lyne, Muckross.*

Billy Vincent, his mother, Maud, and his dog, Sergeant Buzz Fuzz, at Muckross Gardens, 1928. *The Vincent Collection. Courtesy of the Trustees of Muckross House.*

Billy Vincent (1919–2012) outside his boyhood home, Muckross House, in 1998. © *Courtesy of photographer Michelle Cooper Galvin, Killarney.*

Katie Donnelly, Knocknageeha, Gneeveguilla, sole survivor of the Moving Bog tragedy which claimed the lives of eight members of her family on 28 December 1896. *Courtesy of Tom Joe O'Donoghue.*

Tom Joe O'Donoghue, grandson of Katie Donnelly, his son, Padraig, and granddaughter, Michelle, at the site of the Moving Bog monument near Gneeveguilla village. *Courtesy of Kerry's Eye.*

The O'Connell Memorial Church is the only church in Ireland to be called after a lay person. Also called the Holy Cross church, it was the brainchild of Castleisland-born Fr Timothy Brosnan, who became the parish priest of Cahersiveen in 1879. Fund-raising drives among Irish emigrants in North America, Britain and Australia provided much of the funds. Inside the tower door on the Killarney side of the edifice is a four-hundredweight slab of black marble, which originated in the Catacombs of Saint Clement in Rome and was gifted to the new church by Pope Leo XIII. On 1 August 1888 the marble was laid as the cornerstone by Archbishop Croke of Cashel, one of the founders of the GAA. Some will tell you that a steeple was never added to the church because of lack of funds; others will say it was because the church is built on bog and would not take the weight; and more will say the truth lies in a combination of the two versions.

Junior Murphy has another good story about the construction. Two masons are said to have brought a bottle of whiskey to work with them. When the parish priest took them unawares by turning up on the scaffolding for an inspection, one of the masons hastily concealed the bottle with a few trowels of mortar; the bottle of whiskey is believed to be still up there, encased in its plaster cast.

We walked around to the back of the church to see the gravestone of Monsignor Hugh O'Flaherty (1898–1963), whose epitaph is 'God Has No Country'. Monsignor O'Flaherty's daring in Second World War Rome earned him the nickname 'The Scarlet Pimpernel of the Vatican'. With a group of like-minded accomplices, he outwitted the occupying Nazi forces to spirit over 6,500 Allied soldiers and Jews to safety. After the war, he frequently visited German and Italian POWs, including his nemesis Gestapo Chief Colonel Herbert Kappler, to ensure they were treated properly. In 1945 he was made a Commander of the British Empire (CBE) and in 1946 he received the US Medal of Freedom with Silver Palm.

Illness prompted his retirement to Cahersiveen in 1960. He had close connections with the town through his sister, Bridie, who had married a South Kerry man, Christy Sheehan. Monsignor O'Flaherty holidayed regularly at the couple's home in west Main Street, where they ran a general hardware business, and he was very popular in Cahersiveen. He died on 30 October 1963.

If you want to invoke the real spirit of Cahersiveen, you must listen to a rendition of the town's anthem, 'The Boys of Barr na Sráide', which would move a heart of stone, especially when it is sung at funerals.

Oh the town it climbs the mountains,
And looks upon the sea,
And sleeping time or waking time,
It's there I'd like to be.
To walk again those kindly streets
The place I grew a man,
With the Boys of Barr na Sráide
Who hunted for the Wran.

The fine ballad was composed by poet, playwright and short-story writer Sigerson Clifford, who was born in Cork city in

1913 and later moved to Cahersiveen with his parents, Michael Clifford and Mary Anne Sigerson. Originally Eddie Clifford, he later took the pen name Sigerson Clifford. His house has since been demolished, but to understand the full import of the ballad, take a stroll up to his childhood hunting grounds on Top Street, or *Barr na Sráide*, and see how the town really does climb the mountain.

Srugrena Cemetery and the Ballaghasheen Road are signposted to the left of the main Killarney to Cahersiveen Road about two miles from the town. The cemetery was a burial ground for destitute people, termed paupers, many of whom were Famine victims who sought help at Bahaghs Workhouse, which is located about a mile down the road towards Cahersiveen. A local farmer had the contract to bury the dead.

The Great Famine, which began in 1845 and continued for about six years, resulted from the failure of potato crops due to blight. About one million people are estimated to have died while a further two million emigrated. Many Famine victims were buried in mass graves such as the one at Srugrena, overlooking a flat expanse of bogland to the east of Cahersiveen. The echoes in the hillside burial ground, which slopes away from the gate on the Ballaghasheen Road, are a haunting reminder of the countless souls who finally found a resting place here after the torment of empty stomachs and bodies wracked by fever and starvation.

The Irish translation of Srugrena is *sruth gréine*, meaning 'stream of the sun'; another translation is 'the gravelly stream'. Small stones, unhewn and unmarked, pit the scrubby ground, but they are just a token indication of the thousands of men,

women and children from Iveragh who were interred here
without inscriptions to record their time on this earth.

If their departure was anonymous, there have been generous
gestures in recent times to acknowledge their lives. Junior
Murphy records in his book on Cahersiveen that on the 150th
anniversary of the opening of the workhouse, the pupils of the
nearby Coars National School commemorated those laid to rest
in Srugrena. That commemoration took place at the cemetery
on 5 May 1997 and, as part of the ceremony, the owners of the
ruined workhouse, Kathleen and James O'Sullivan, donated a
granite stone which had originally served as the altar of the
building's chapel. The altar slab, sculpted and engraved with
an inscription in Gaelic, was set in the cemetery to serve as a
communal gravestone for the Famine victims. The inscription
translates as 'Pray for all us souls who died in the Great Famine
and are buried in this graveyard.'

Travelling down the road from Srugrena towards the main
Cahersiveen to Killarney Road, you will see the imposing walls
and roofless structure of Bahaghs Workhouse rising to the left.
Bahaghs, or *Beathach* in Irish, translates as birchy land. If you
were not aware of its grim history, the workhouse has all the
appearance of a grand country house, with a façade boasting
impressive architectural features. Located three miles to the
east of Cahersiveen, it was originally called Bahoss House.
According to Valerie Bary, Bahoss was built in about 1833
by Charles O'Connell on his marriage to Kate O'Connell,
favourite daughter of the Liberator, Daniel O'Connell. But the
couple were to fall on hard times and 'Charles and Kate were
forced eventually to leave their beautiful home which showed

a sophistication and affluence little known in Iveragh', Bary writes.

The development of the workhouse and its administration is detailed by Junior Murphy in his book. Purchased in 1842 on foot of the Poor Law Acts of the 1830s and the 1840s, the lodge was developed into Bahaghs Workhouse. The Cahersiveen Relief Committee provided £8,850 to finance the construction work, which took three years. Workers were paid nine old pence a day. The workhouse was built of mortar and faced with red-brick, which is still evident today. There were granite cornerstones and Valentia slate window sills and lintels.

The workhouse took in its first inmates on 17 October 1846. It had a planned capacity of 400, but at the height of the Famine, on 10 February 1848, there were 1,241 residents. There were also nine auxiliary workhouses in the region. The former Cahersiveen Library and a number of adjacent houses all served as workhouses during the Famine. The workhouse consisted of a chapel, hospital, school, washhouse, residence, soup kitchen and mortuary. There were three storeys, the top storey serving as the hospital, the middle section the staff quarters and the first floor the sleeping area. Breakfast consisted of eight ounces of Indian corn and naggins of rice mix. Soup was served for dinner with sixteen ounces of bread.

Leaving behind Bahaghs, described by Valerie Bary as a 'house of considerable atmosphere', Junior and I passed a boreen on the right-hand side as we headed towards Cahersiveen. Junior explained that this was *Bóthar na mBocht*, the Road of the Poor, known locally as Paupers' Road. The desperation of those who walked this road to the workhouse is beyond imagining.

Back on the main road, a short distance along to the right, we saw the little memorial park on the banks of the River Carhan marking the birthplace of Daniel O'Connell in 1775. His father was Morgan O'Connell, one of twenty-two children, and his mother was Catherine, a native of Whitechurch near Blarney in County Cork. The family owned 600 acres when O'Connell was born. The ruins of the home place lie on private ground on the far bank of the river.

Valentia: A World Apart

Valentia Island is a world apart; so much so that, in 1828, the 18th Knight of Kerry, Maurice Fitzgerald, was of the opinion that there was no good reason why, as an island completely cut off from the mainland of south-west Kerry at that time, Valentia should not have its independence. He planned to use his position as a Westminster MP to introduce a Bill that would make Valentia an independent county. His view was that the island economy would perform better economically if it were separated from the rest of Kerry for administrative purposes.

The Knight's 'highly unusual campaign' was the subject of an article in the Tralee newspaper, *Chute's Western Herald*, on Monday 1 December 1828. The paper reported that many people were of the opinion that Valentia would soon become a 'packet station' for ships linking North America and Ireland and also that a railroad would be built from Dublin to Valentia Harbour. The *Chute's* journalist made the following prediction: 'We do not know if the Knight is entirely serious in his campaign to give Ireland an extra county, but we believe that great things may yet happen in Valentia Island.'

The article proved prophetic, at least in the sense that a railroad opened on 12 September 1893, the Great Southern and Western Railway running from Farranfore to Reenard Point on Valentia Harbour. Neither the packet station nor 'County Valentia' materialised, but a bridge linking Portmagee to the island opened in 1970, reducing the isolation of the islanders to a significant degree. The island's other connection to the mainland is a car ferry running between Reenard Point and Knightstown, a planned village with a distinctly English appearance.

Among the 'great things' that did come to pass on Valentia was the advent, in 1866, of the Transatlantic Cable link, which was in its day a communications revolution akin to the introduction of the Internet. After a number of abortive attempts to lay the cable between Newfoundland and Valentia, *The Great Eastern*, which was one of the first ever iron ships, succeeded in laying the cable right across the sea bed between the two continents in 1866. While the ship has long since disappeared, its top mast now serves as the giant flagpole at Anfield, Liverpool Football Club's grounds. The mast was salvaged when the ship was broken up for scrap at Rock Ferry on the River Mersey by Henry Bath & Sons Ltd in 1888–90.

The markedly British influence on Valentia, or *Oileán Dairbhre*, the Island of the Oaks, is due to a combination of ventures that led to an influx of people: the cable station, the lighthouse, the slate quarry and Valentia Observatory. But the overarching influence on its development was the zeal of successive knights of Kerry.

In her book on the island, Nellie O'Cleirigh writes that Maurice Fitzgerald kept up his connections with government even after he lost his Westminster seat and used them where possible to get favours for Valentia and 'incidentally for himself'. He wrote constantly to the Prime Minister, the Duke of Wellington. When, in 1830, he engaged Alexander Nimmo to design the new village, Knightstown, directly across the water from Reenard Point, he named the front walk by the sea 'Wellington Place'. Much of the history of Knightstown lies beneath an immaculate surface; take, for instance the large stone drains leading down to the sea, wide enough to take a man. Here is the story recounted to me by my island guide, Michael Egan, a Mayo man who came to work in the island's coastguard radio station and never left.

Halfway up the hill on the left-hand side of the street is a two-storey house, fronted with a large flat-roofed extension. It formerly operated as an RIC barracks with a basement jail. Two locals imprisoned in the jail discovered a large stone drain opening out of it and escaped down to the seafront. One of them took a boat to the mainland, continued on to Scotland and never returned. The second remained on the island and married.

That basement still exists under what is now the home of

the Walsh family, who ran a grocery from the building until 1994. Tony Walsh (aged ninety-two), introduced to me by Michael, emigrated to England as a young man and returned in 1948, opening his shop in Knightstown the following year and running it with his brother, Diarmuid. Knightstown had a thriving grocery trade in the 1950s and 1960s; the other grocers besides the Walshs were O'Sullivan, O'Driscoll and Reidy, which is still trading at the time of writing. There was also Tailor Casey's shop and Miss Murphy's. In addition to the native islanders, business was generated by the twenty-three houses of the cable station, the lighthouse keepers and the radio station. 'There was a sergeant and four guards, two churches and two doctors,' Tony recalled.

Nellie O'Cleirigh remarks that when Valentia was at its most prosperous, in the early 1900s, Knightstown had a good hotel, the cable station, the slate yard, two churches, a hospital, a courthouse, a jail, a police barracks, a Mason's Lodge, a Fisherman's Hall and several prosperous shops, including a bakery. Walsh's shop got a delivery of fresh confectionery twice a week from the train at Reenard Point. Thompson's bakery sent cardboard boxes of its bread and cakes down on the train to Cahersiveen. 'People were queuing up for them,' Tony said. He had a hand-barrow to collect goods from the ferry and eventually replaced it with a barrow with an engine. He was coming up the hill one day when he met a guard who told him to get tax and insurance for the barrow.

Tony remembers going to the Blasket Islands on an excursion of three boats from Valentia. 'I knew Peig Sayers,' he said. 'I danced in her kitchen. We nearly got lost coming home.

Halfway through dancing a set, we got called away – the weather got bad. We got an awful doing going home.' While he was working as a temporary lighthouse keeper at Tearaght Lighthouse off the Dingle Peninsula in about 1940, Tony witnessed the bombing of a British ship, the SS *Latymer*. 'There was a ship going towards the rock, and an aeroplane came along and bombed it out,' he said. 'Six died, and the others were brought in here. The skipper was in the hospital. She sank four hours after being bombed. I watched every minute of it. She was exploding every minute.'

Across the street from Walshs', and a little further up the hill, is an attractive red and white building, Knightstown Coffee Shop, which has the year 1888 on the façade. This building, formerly owned by the O'Sullivan family, was once a hotel, bakery, shop and off-licence. The meat sold by the O'Sullivans came from their slaughterhouse located in nearby Jane Street. The former slaughterhouse has been transformed into a flower-bedecked stone cottage. Michael shows me the deep channels running at the foot of the walls, a reminder of a more grisly past when blood flowed through them.

Jane Street and Peter Street, across the way from it, were said to be called after members of the Knight of Kerry's family, but this is a matter of debate. At the end of Peter Street is a terrace of coastguard houses, Coastal Terrace, overlooking Beginish Island and the mainland. Also on Peter Street is St Deararca's Hall, called after the island's patron saint, who was reputed to be a sister of St Patrick. The hall, which dates back to 1906, was the island's 'Ballroom of Romance' for many years.

The imposing landmark on the seafront in Knightstown is

the clock tower, again a project of the Knight of Kerry. It was restored in recent years by the island's Tidy Towns Committee which is headed up by Michael Egan. Valentia Tidy Towns also restored 'The Rocket Car', which was used to shoot cables to stricken vessels as part of sea rescues between 1902 and 1989. The brightly painted timber car is now housed on the water's edge in the former waiting room for the ferry.

A little further down the road is a terrace of cable-station houses. Michael explained how the houses were way ahead of their time in terms of construction:

> They were built for the Western Union workers. They were possibly the first houses in Ireland to have cavity walls. They were also built of brick brought over from England to Reenard Point where they were again transported by boat to the present site. The locals were the builders of these houses and as a result these locals were in big demand on the mainland because of their cavity skills and their brickwork skills. By the best of standards today, I would say these houses are still away ahead of their time.

Building skills of a different kind are evident in the old lifeboat station which stands behind the modern station just beyond the town clock. Built in 1864 at Reenard Point, the whole structure was dismantled in 1869 and rebuilt stone for stone in its present location. The apartment development behind the old lifeboat station was once the site of a huge coal shed used to bunker the ships calling to the harbour. The coal was weighed in front of the town clock. Beside the coal shed was a large timber yard.

Beyond the apartments is Reenellen House, once the home

of the self-taught marine biologist Maude Delap and her family, who moved there from the rectory on the death of her father, a Church of Ireland clergyman. The garden is overrun with giant *Gunnera*, which resembles rhubarb, and the house, though still roofed, is in a sorry state of dereliction.

From this lower end of the village we walked back up to the top and took a right turn at the end of the line of buildings, almost directly opposite the Church of Ireland, to the workplace of the sculptor Alan Ryan Hall, who is responsible for most of the statues along the Ring of Kerry, from the bust of Daniel O'Connell at Carhan outside Cahersiveen to the statue of the wrestler Steve Casey in Sneem. For years Alan has left a small gallery open to the public; donations to the Valentia Hospital are invited in lieu of an entrance fee. The gallery houses several examples of the artist's work and is worth a visit, especially for examples of his subversive sense of humour.

A little further down this laneway is Atlantic Villa, a guesthouse run by Brian and Jackie Morgan, originally built in 1873 as the residence of the first Superintendent of the Western Union Cable Station, James Graves, who was born on 4 August 1833 at Chesterton near Cambridge. The pitch pine in the house was brought over from Heart's Content in Newfoundland along with the cable.

A short distance from Knightstown is Glanleam House and Gardens, once the home of the Knight of Kerry, who converted the building, originally a linen mill dating back to 1775. And no visit to Valentia is complete without a visit to the Heritage Centre, which is located in an old schoolhouse just beyond the Church of Ireland in Knightstown. A series of exhibitions in the centre narrate the fascinating aspects of the island's history, including the famous slate quarry, the advent of the cable, sea rescues and rowing successes.

The Misses Delap

The Cahersiveen train slows to a crawl on the steep incline overlooking the Atlantic and a young boy jumps out to sprint alongside it, steam billowing past him. His two sisters, caught between excitement and alarm at his daring, call out the window to him. They are on their way to Valentia Island, a glorious summer of freedom stretching ahead of them and a stifling year of boarding school in England behind them. Crossing from Reenard Point on the ferry, they can glimpse their aunts, Maude and Connie, waiting on the pier in Knightstown with the donkey and car to carry their luggage. Above in Reenellen House, with its exotic smell of 'soup and formalin', Aunt Mary and the housekeeper, Mrs Kate Dore, will be preparing food for the three youngsters, Peter, Molly and Anne, whose family is based in Dublin but who are in boarding school because of the overseas postings of their father, George Delap, a doctor with the Royal Army Medical Corps. Although it is the late 1920s, the children step into an Edwardian world when they walk through the gate of Reenellen House and into the lives of their three maiden aunts who wear ankle-length skirts and dresses.

Today, the name Delap remains very much alive on Valentia Island, chiefly because of the memory of Maude Delap (1866–1953), a self-taught marine biologist referred to as the 'jellyfish lady' because of her scientific studies of the complex life cycle of the species. In the Valentia Heritage Centre in Knightstown her microscope and sketchbooks are on display. Here you can also read how, in 1935, Professor Thomas Alan Stephenson named a new species of sea anemone *Edwardsia delapiae* after Maude, who had discovered it.

Maude's story is intrinsically bound up with that of her elder sister, Mary (1865–1938); her younger sister, Constance, better known as Connie (1868–1935); and Mrs Kate Dore from Peter Street, Knightstown, who was an integral part of the family. Mrs Dore's husband, John, was the mechanic for the Valentia lifeboat. The three sisters were part of a family of ten children: Mary, Maud, Constance, Flora, Anna, Everine, William, Alexander, Alfred and George.

Descendant Joanna Lee of Dublin inherited memories of the Reenellen household from relatives, including her late mother, Molly Friel, and from conversations with her aunt, Anne Delap, who was aged ninety-two in 2013. Joanna drew on these conversations and on family memories when I interviewed her in 2013. She said, 'Mary was the boss, she told you what had to be done, and Maude was the organiser, who got it done. Connie was the gentle one, the motherly one who comforted you. Mary ran things and kept the other two in order. Maude was the one who was fun and informative.' The sisters read *The Irish Times*, played the piano and lived a Spartan lifestyle in the damp and draughty house, lit with oil lamps and inadequately heated with turf fires.

Their stoic endurance and altruistic love were among the qualities that impressed the late Peter Delap, who relates, in an essay given to me by Joanna, how the family unit came to fragment with the passage of years. 'Sadly, successively, Aunt Connie and Aunt Mary died, Maude soldiering on alone, even managing to keep the lovely, highly productive garden they had created from falling into total wilderness. Throughout these closing years, her main support came from the indomitable Mrs Dore,' he wrote.

In the essay, Peter records that Mrs Dore, a 'huge, stalwart lady', had repaid his aunts in full for the kindness of employing her in hard times. 'I can still hear the slap of her big, bare feet as she came up the stone passages, entered the drawing-room like a dowager duchess and, drawing up a chair beside Aunt Mary, sat down to impart some important news, ignoring the rest of us.' When Mary was dying, Mrs Dore, wrapped in a shawl, would sit for hours outside the bedroom door, 'drawing on a little clay pipe, and ever alert for any sound from within'.

The Delaps were descended from Hugh Delap, who settled in Sligo around 1600 and became a merchant. Their father was Revd Alexander Delap (1830–1906) and their mother was Anna Jane Goslett (1831–1914). In 1876 Revd Delap transferred from Donegal to Kerry to become rector of Valentia Island and Cahersiveen. The family travelled by train, while he brought all their belongings down the west coast by boat. The furniture arrived in a battered condition. John Barlee, a grand-nephew of the sisters, recalled being told in the 1930s and 1940s not to sit on certain chairs because 'their legs were a bit loose from the journey'. 'Maude was ten when she moved from Donegal to Valentia and it must have made a great impression on her,' he said.

Maude and her siblings were influenced by their father's lifelong passion for the sea. His superior, Bishop Graves of Limerick, grandfather of the poet Robert Graves, called him 'my old man of the sea'. He was proud to have the Skelligs in his parish and visited the lighthouse in boats powered simply by oar and sail. Revd Delap was also a keen naturalist, an interest which he transferred to his children and which has persisted right down through the generations. Journalist Anne Byrne, in her book on Irish women scientists and pioneers, wrote that despite Maude's father's liberal leanings, she received no formal education.

Peter Delap remembers early expeditions to the 'back of the island' with Maude. 'She was an old-school Victorian all-round naturalist. A recognised expert on marine biology but also interested in the birds, plants and the archaeology of the whole countryside. We learned so very much from her.' From 1894 up to 1949, when she was eighty-three, Maude continued to send specimens of insects and marine life to the Natural History Museum in Dublin.

Connie shared Maude's interest in marine life; Byrne describes her as an active naturalist who co-wrote two papers on the plankton of the harbour with Maude and collected specimens with her. 'In the late 1890s Valentia was chosen to be the site for a detailed marine study,' Byrne writes. 'The choice was based, in part, it seems, on work by Maude, her sister Constance and their father.' In 1895 Edward T. Browne, of University College London, arrived on Valentia with a team of naturalists to conduct the jellyfish or *medusae* study, which, according to Byrne, was mostly based on tow-nettings by the Delap sisters. 'In fact, the whole survey would probably have been impossible without their help.' Their tow-nettings continued from October 1896 to December 1898, and the sisters sent over a hundred bottles of specimens to Browne, the material forming the basis for many of the survey's reports.

After Revd Delap died in 1906, his widow and three unmarried daughters moved to Reenellen. (Islanders had keened at his funeral, evidence of his great charity to people of all faiths.) Byrne reports that Maude had been offered a post in the Marine Biological Station in Plymouth some time before 1906, but, according to John Barlee, Revd Delap had declared, 'No daughter of mine will leave home except as a married woman.'

For a woman so like a Jane Austen heroine, Maude Delap was not without a love interest, which, in her case, washed up on the island in the person of 'Mr Browne' with whom she had so much in common. Sadly, her love for him appears to have been unrequited because he went on to marry a colleague of his, Margaret Robinson. Despite the marriage, each year, beginning in 1896 and ending only with Edward Browne's death in 1937, Maude sent him a box of violets for his birthday. They also corresponded for over forty years, each letter beginning and ending with the appellations, 'My dear Miss Delap' and 'Yours sincerely, Edward T. Browne', and 'My dear Mr Browne' and 'Yours very sincerely, Maude J. Delap'.

Though the tide ebbed on her scientific collaboration with Browne, Maude continued her work and, in the early 1900s, experimented with raising jellyfish at home in 'the department', which Peter Delap described as a 'heroic jumble of books, specimens, aquaria, with its pervasive low-tide smell'. Molly Friel recalled the smell of preservatives and the sound of oxygen bubbling in the bell jars with the pale mauve jellyfish swimming around inside. The creak of the oar locks as Maude rowed out to Doulus Head reverberated down through the years in the mind of Anne Gore, who recalled their sound in her Belfast home in 2013. Peter remembered 'endless idyllic hours' trolling for pollock and mackerel in the brown punt until full summer darkness; the fish were shared in the 'unbounded hospitality' of the aunts. He paints a wonderful picture of those sea outings:

> Sometimes the summer dark was enlivened by the outward passage of the local seine boats in search of the big mackerel shoals. Up to a dozen boats would pass, racing each other with shouts and song and always underneath the short, stabbing chop of the oars; it had all the exhilaration of a Viking raid, without the peril.

The social conscience of the three aunts was demonstrated through running the Fishermens' Hall on the island and their voluntary work at Valentia Hospital. 'Incidentally, my Aunt Mary was perhaps the last living person to pronounce it 'orspital in the eighteenth-century mode, perhaps out of deference to her father, her diction being otherwise infinitely precise,' Peter recalled. Through their charity, the aunts were following in the footsteps of their father, who had worked hand in hand with the

Catholic parish priest to alleviate the poverty of the islanders. Once asked by his granddaughter, Rhonda, what were 'the Catholics', Revd Delap had replied, 'Never ask me that, child, we are all God's children.'

Following the deaths of Mary and Connie, Maude stayed on at Reenellen, tending the fruit and vegetable garden right into her old age. Anne Byrne describes her as a 'prodigious gardener growing peaches, grapes and washed-up seeds and nuts in a tumbledown greenhouse'. She also generated a little money from growing arum lilies and a small white gladiolus called 'The Bride', which were sent by train to Dublin. The ever-faithful Mrs Dore was her constant support in her declining years.

A Celtic Tiger-style housing development has grown up around Reenellen, casting it adrift like an apparition from another era. The garden is overrun, and, though the roof of the house is still intact, the building is derelict. Below it, the sea washes the little beach from where Maude and Connie Delap set out on their voyages of discovery, the oar locks creaking in time with their strokes.

Derrynane Journeys

In an era of travel by horse on roads little better than rutted mountain tracks, Daniel O'Connell's journeys up and down nineteenth-century Ireland were extremely demanding. Known as 'the Liberator', the Kerryman's greatest achievement was winning Catholic Emancipation in 1829. His statue stands on Dublin's O'Connell Street in recognition of this, and in James Joyce's short story 'The Dead', Gabriel salutes it, saying, 'Good night, Dan.' O'Connell was also famed as a barrister on the court circuit. His legal and political careers both conspired to keep him on the rutted roads of Ireland for long stretches.

Although he had taken a house on Dublin's Merrion Square, the family seat, Derrynane House, was perched on the wild Atlantic seaboard of the Iveragh Peninsula. In his day this indescribably beautiful corner of South Kerry could only be reached by negotiating a series of mountain passes and wild valleys or by boat. The persistence of the Irish language in Iveragh long after it had declined in other parts of Kerry is often given as an indication of its isolation. Its remoteness was conveyed by the Cork author Seán Ó Faoláin in the following passage:

> That rainswept, hungry peninsula, jagging out into the Atlantic, can never be thought of as lovely as long as we remember that it was – even on its brightest days – as hard as the welts on the hands of the women and the men; as lonely as a cock-crow; as utterly lost to the world – lost, apart from its rent roll, even to Dublin, with its sham parliament – as some slave plantation in the Carolinas.

The weather-slated Derrynane House was inherited by Daniel O'Connell from his smuggler uncle, Maurice 'Hunting Cap' O'Connell, who traded illicitly in rum, silks, lace, wines, tea, brandy and sugar. Its remoteness did not deter international visitors from seeking the Liberator out on home turf, among them a German aristocrat and famed author, Prince Hermann von Pückler-Muskau, who arrived on horseback at Derrynane late one night in September 1828. The prince, who was famed as a travel writer, spent two nights in O'Connell's home at the sea's edge and penned a lyrical description of his surroundings, including the nearby Ballinskelligs Bay. 'Truly it is a land of the eagle and the vulture, of the stormy wave and the rugged rock,' he wrote.

The Irish Ambassador to Germany, Dan Mulhall, who delivered a lecture on 'King Dan and the German Prince' in Derrynane in August 2012, said the fact that the Prince made the long journey from Wicklow to Derrynane pointed to the Kerryman's reputation in Europe at the time. The Ambassador noted, 'The Prince thought that O'Connell looked more like a general in Napoleon's army than a Dublin advocate. He found him to be witty and persuasive in manner rather than loftily eloquent.' When the German took his leave of Derrynane, O'Connell rode part of the way with him and the two men parted 'at the ruins of a bridge carried away by the swelling of a mountain stream'.

When O'Connell's illustrious legal career of some thirty years had all but drawn to a close in 1829, he withdrew to Derrynane, where, in the words of Seán Ó Faoláin, he became 'reinvigorated by the mountain air, chased the mountain hares, and drank in the spirit of his land from the wild loveliness of his home'. The demands of a career based on small cases – Catholics were still restricted from rising to the rank of King's Counsel or judge

– meant that he had been forced to travel continually around the country to practise in several court circuits. Entrenched in Derrynane once again, he was loath to put his feet in the stirrups to travel any great journey. But there was to be one notable exception and one remarkable journey for one celebrated case. Mr Justice Adrian Hardiman of the Irish Supreme Court, in an address to the O'Connell Heritage Summer School in Derrynane on 7 September 2013, described this case as 'one of the most celebrated of O'Connell's legal triumphs because it was his swansong as a practising barrister'.

At the start of the summer of 1829, O'Connell was asked to defend twenty-one men accused of the Doneraile Conspiracy in County Cork, but he refused. Arising out of a background of tensions between tenants and landowners in North Cork, the men were accused of a conspiracy to shoot three members of the upper classes, George Bond Lowe, Michael Creagh and Rear-Admiral Evans. Hardiman suggests that O'Connell refused the case because he was 'worn out after the events of the year and the twenty-five years of ceaseless agitation which had preceded it'.

The trial began on 21 October 1829, and the first four men before the Cork Court were convicted and sentenced to death by hanging. Meanwhile, down in Kerry, O'Connell was disporting himself, in the words of Ó Faoláin, 'like a petty German king, with his hounds, his early-morning hunting, his red-coated men with their long staves hallooing from glen to glen'. But Ó Faoláin went on to relate how, even there, his people dragged him from his retreat. One Sunday morning at eight o'clock, 'he looked out to the sound of a horse's hoofs, and saw Burke of Ballyhea staggering to the door after an all-night ride of ninety miles'. At Burke's entreaty, O'Connell set out for Cork immediately, beginning a journey that has lost none of its drama in the intervening years.

William Burke, a brother of one of those yet to be tried, left Cork on the evening of Saturday 24 October 1829 to ride to Derrynane and to arrange for relays of horses for O'Connell's journey back to Cork. 'A considerable part of the fame of the trial relates to this heroic ride and O'Connell's subsequent drive in his gig to arrive in Cork about 10 o'clock on the morning of the Monday,' Ó Faoláin said. He evokes a picture of O'Connell driving alone 'across the wild passes, through Glenshesk [sic] and Ballyvourney ... beside the sleeping hamlets the rustle of the mountains streams, down the smoother valleys of the Lee – nearer and nearer to the city, with Burke galloping ahead of him to bring the news'. He imagined the moon paling over the Lee, the roofs of Cork rising out of its little smoky valley and the tired horseman sighing, 'Alas, in from all that heart-lifting beauty to the rascality of an Irish court of justice.' Hardiman described the epic 90-mile journey through the night as 'no mean achievement for a corpulent man in his fifty-fifth year'.

Covered with the mud and dust of the roads, O'Connell rushed into the courtroom and asked leave to drink a bowl of milk while he was being briefed. Almost at once, he was on his feet, arguing, 'his mouth full of milk and meat'. To quote the advocate's words from another famous case, he went on to 'drive a coach and four' through the prosecution's tainted evidence, earning an acquittal for his clients after the jury, locked up for thirty-six hours without food, could not agree. The first batch of four, who had been tried before O'Connell took on the case, were reprieved.

An account of another of O'Connell's journeys, one more sociable than dramatic, has come down to us through the diary of an Englishman, Henry Crabb Robinson, who was born in the same year as the Liberator and who visited Ireland in 1826. D. L. Kelleher, writing in the 1920s, relates how Robinson travelled from Cork to Killarney with O'Connell in the top seat of the 'post-car'. O'Connell 'squeezed up to give him room with as much welcome as it were for a favourite child'. Kelleher paints this picture of the politician: 'O'Connell talks now with a sparkling kind of gaiety; these jaunts home are always his relaxations. After the comparative pose and strut of the courts, he uses a gentler magnetism and becomes just the jolly, vivid half-Latin Irishman of the south.'

Robinson related that on arrival in Killarney they switched to 'an outside car – a Russian droshky, in fact – a by no means inconvenient vehicle on good roads'. On the last section of the journey, both men ride horses through O'Connell territory, and 'many tenants run alongside, keeping up with the horses, and arguing their cases while they run'. At journey's end in Derrynane, Robinson remarked on the eagerness with which O'Connell 'sprang from his horse and kissed a toothless old woman, his nurse'.

The Gun-runner

The skull on display in the side porch of the Franciscan friary in Killarney had been in the possession of the family of Daniel O'Connell in Derrynane for about two centuries when it was mysteriously removed (some say stolen) in 1847. Bizarrely, it was returned anonymously by post via Winchester in 1931 and was presented to the Killarney friars a decade later. Given the drama that surrounded the movements of the relic, the energies of the eventful life of Fr Francis O'Sullivan, known as the Scariff Martyr, did not appear to have dissipated with his death.

As with the most interesting of characters, the Franciscan embodied some apparent contradictions in his personality. A pious and a prayerful man, he nonetheless could have been described as a gun-runner or a subversive; he orchestrated the smuggling of a frigate of muskets and ammunition from Spain into Ireland in 1642. Such activities obviously did not endear him to the Cromwellian forces, who hunted him down in his native South Kerry over a decade later. He was killed on Scariff Island, within sight of Derrynane Harbour, apparently while saying Mass.

There is some debate about the actual location in South Kerry of his birthplace, and the fact that two townlands on either side of Kenmare Bay claim him is probably an indication of his significance. Writing in *Tuosist 6000*, Fr Tomás B. Ó Luanaigh explores the martyr's connection with Ardea on the

Kenmare side of the bay. Fr Ó Luanaigh holds that O'Sullivan was born at Kineagh in the parish of Waterville on the opposite side of the bay in 1591 and that his connection with Ardea was through his father, Moriarty O'Sullivan. Moriarty was head of the Kineagh section of the family based in Iveragh but belonged to the Ardea division of the O'Sullivans, known as the O'Sullivan Tanist. Fr Ó Luanaigh acknowledges that two other writers, Sr Philomena McCarthy and T. J. Barrington, claim the parish of Tuosist as O'Sullivan's birthplace since there is evidence of the O'Sullivan clan bearing the nickname *Ceannach* in Kenmare and nearby Tuosist. (Kineagh translates as *ceann each*, the head of the horse.)

Historian Gerard Lyne explained that the tánaiste or tanist was the 'chosen one', elected during the lifetime of the reigning chieftain, to succeed him. In the case of O'Sullivan Beare, the seat of the reigning chieftain was Dunboy in west Cork, and that of his tánaiste the castle of Ardea, in the parish of Tuosist, County Kerry.

O'Sullivan's baptismal name was Diarmuid, but he took the name Francis when he became a friar in Spain. Fr Ó Luanaigh relates that he was known alternately as 'Father Caneach', as 'an Bráthair Rua' (the Red Brother) and as 'Bráthair Rua na Scairbe' (the Red Brother of Scariff).

Fr O'Sullivan was a nephew of Rickard (or Richard) O'Connell, who became Bishop of Ardfert in September 1641 and was consecrated in June 1643. Like many of his contemporaries, O'Sullivan was truly European in his outlook, having been educated in Spain and Italy at a time when this was the only academic option for Irish Catholics from influential families. Having studied the humanities and theology in Spain, where he was ordained a priest, O'Sullivan moved to Italy. According to Fr Patrick Conlan, OFM, author of *Irish Franciscans in the Nineteenth Century*, his admittance to the newly founded Saint Isidore's College in Rome is recorded under the date 8 April 1626.

He returned to Kerry around 1630 to preach and to hear confessions. In 1636 he was guardian of one of three friaries located in Ardfert and by 1649 he was a guardian in Timoleague, County Cork.

The following description of his character by the Capuchin, Fr Robert O'Connell, also from Desmond, is given in Fr Conlan's book: 'a dignified, modest, and pious man, whose very countenance showed him to be a genuine son of St Francis'. In 1641 this pious Kerryman was back in Spain, entreating King Philip to come to the aid of his persecuted countrymen. He appears to have won the ear and the sympathy of the King.

According to Fr Cathaldus Giblin, OFM, in *Daniel O'Connell and the Irish Franciscans*, Fr O'Sullivan had been chosen by the Munster chiefs during the course of the 1641 rebellion to plead the cause of their 'distracted country' at the Spanish court and his mission was 'entirely successful'. The ensuing financial aid and armaments were listed by Fr Giblin: '£3,000 in plate silver coins, four demie canons, his own for each province, 2,500 muskets with their addresses, 300 barrels of powder, matche bullet and pickes accordingly.'

By 1650 Fr O'Sullivan was Provincial of the Irish Franciscans and a wanted man in Kerry, where the Penal Laws were in full force. At this time he was also appointed Professor of Theology by the Bishop of Kerry at the short-lived theological college in Tralee. Despite the campaign of persecution being waged by the forces of Cromwell, the courageous and patriotic friar continued to minister to his people in South Kerry. Perhaps he felt safer there among his kinspeople at the edge of the ocean and in the mountainous landscape where he had first seen the light of day.

The events leading up to his violent death are set out as follows by Fr Conlan. During the ravaging of Kerry by the Cromwellian soldiers under Colonel Nelson in June 1653, the local Irish went into hiding in the mountains, in the woods and in the caves. One such group, with the Franciscan Provincial, was discovered – tradition says on the island of Scariff and while Fr O'Sullivan was saying Mass. On 23 June O'Sullivan was put to death. The friar's burial place is not known. According to Fr Ó Luanaigh, he was buried on Scariff Island and later reinterred at Derrynane by the O'Connells, who were friendly with the Franciscans. He further adds, 'The O'Connells had apparently used this sacred relic as a respected substitute for the Bible when solemn oaths were to be sworn.' T. J. Barrington relates in his book, *Discovering Kerry*, that a portion of the skull became an important relic for the O'Connells, and in the time of Daniel O'Connell's uncle, 'Hunting Cap', oaths were sworn on it. 'It was the practice of the local fishermen to invoke his aid in these stormy and dangerous seas,' according to the author.

The passage of the centuries has all but eroded any appreciation of the adventures of the South Kerry man whose horizons extended to the court of Spain and the antique splendour of Rome, and whose concern for the plight of his people spurred him to supply them with Spanish arms as well as ministering to their souls. But his day may dawn again. The case for the canonisation of Fr O'Sullivan, *An Bráthair Rua*, was formally presented to Rome in 1998, together with the cases of fellow Kerry martyrs Dominican Fr Thaddeus Moriarty, OP, Tralee, and Fr Conor McCarthy, PP, Killeentierna, Currow.

Albinia's Jewels

A ristocrat Albinia Brodrick turned her back on English society life in the early years of the twentieth century to devote herself to alleviating poverty in Kerry as a nurse. A series of roofless, stone buildings overlooking the sea outside the village of Castlecove, between Sneem and Waterville on the Ring of Kerry road, are an enduring reminder of the strong-willed daughter of Viscount Midleton, who went against conventional wisdom to build a hospital miles from any urban centre.

The complex of buildings beside West Cove pier, christened Ballincoona, or *Baile an Chúnaimh*, meaning 'home of help', was nearing completion in 1914, with accommodation for twenty-two patients. In a 1914 report, referred to by local historian T. E. Stoakley in his book on Sneem, Albinia is quoted: 'It was cheering to us to have the verdict of the Matron from one of the greatest London hospitals that Ballincoona compares favourably in up-to-date arrangements with the newest Metropolitan Hospitals.' Yet, the author reports, the hospital project came to nothing and had 'started on the road to dereliction even before it had been used'. Factors he cites for its failure were the War of Independence and the Civil War and the gradual withdrawal of English and Anglo-Irish support as Albinia's republican views became known. The peer's daughter, who was then in her forties, ultimately failed with the hospital, but she did run a profitable co-operative shop on the same 16-acre holding she had bought in 1908 under the aegis of the Congested District Board. One local is quoted by Stoakley as follows: 'She had household goods; groceries. She had a bit of drapery. She had fertilizers for the land. She'd a bit of everything.'

The unlikely republican, born in London on 16 December 1861, was the fifth daughter of William Brodrick, the 8th Viscount Midleton, who owned the town of Midleton, County Cork, and much of the land around it. As a young woman, she was a regular visitor to Buckingham Palace, but she developed a strong social conscience, stating in 1903 after a visit to Ireland, 'Overall is a sense of poverty lying as a weight, the poverty of the real poor.' Between 1901 and 1904 she trained as a nurse, and, while training as a midwife in Dublin in 1908, she became involved in the Gaelic League.

The late Pádraig Ó Loinsigh from Ballylongford, County Cork, interviewed several residents of Castlecove and Caherdaniel who had worked for Albinia Brodrick and shared memories of her. He wrote that locals remembered her as Lady Brodrick, a title she did not hold. Others referred to her as Miss Brodrick, but her admirers would like her to be remembered as

Gobnait Ní Bhruadair. She was the sister of Lord Midleton, leader of the Unionists in the South, who negotiated the Truce in 1921, but when asked if he was her brother her reply was 'He used to be my brother.'

Ó Loinsigh noted that the Curran family on Deenish Island in Derrynane Bay were Albinia's hosts for six months, where she learned to speak Irish with an upper-class English accent and changed her name to Gobnait Ní Bhruadair. Reflecting the undying interest in this feisty radical, Kerry Archaeological and Historical Society hosted a talk by Pádraig Ó Concubhair in February 2013. He related that, when queried as to the advisability of locating a hospital in such a remote area as Castlecove, Albinia replied, 'Did you ever need to be driven eighteen miles with a fractured thigh? Has your wife bled to death for want of treatment? Has your child gone lame for want of treatment?' He held that though the hospital cost £11,000 and never really functioned, Gobnait Ní Bhruadair did make a difference: 'Many people in Castlecove had reason to be grateful to Gobnait, as the presence of a trained nurse and midwife was a great benefit to the community.' He quoted a headline in the *Daily Mail*: 'Peer's Sister Sells Her Jewels and Lives on 5s a Week: Remarkable Self-Sacrifice of a Society Lady'.

In the aftermath of the 1916 Rising, which had affected her deeply, Gobnait became a member of Sinn Féin and Cumann na mBan. Stories of her fearless and resourceful spirit are legion. Ó Concubhair related how the late Dean Charles Gray-Stack (1912–85), who served as Church of Ireland rector in Kenmare, recalled her taking up a collection at a dinner party in Sneem for 'our girls in the glasshouse', a reference to female republican prisoners. Thinking that she was referring to 'fallen women', the genteel guests donated generously.

Stoakley gives a detailed account of how, when she was about sixty, Gobnait was shot by a soldier in a convoy of Crossley troop-carriers which she had attempted to delay by cycling in the middle of the road. Her fiery spirit bridled at what she saw as a lack of recognition of the role of women in the War of Independence and the Civil War, as expressed in references to republican speeches made in Countess Road, Killarney, during the 1930s:

> There were many tributes to the men who fought throughout the two wars. Of the women who made those fights possible by their work, there was no recognition. Hewers of wood and drawers of water – good enough for women. It is time that women stood up and claimed their rightful place in Irish history.

On a more pedestrian note, a long-standing helper at Ballincoona related to Stoakley how Gobnait expected her workers to adhere to her vegetarian principles: 'No bit of meat from God or the world would she give them ... But she used to look after them all like that, but it was all peas and beans and things like that she used to give them, you see.'

At the age of eighty-three, she decided to close the hospital building in Castlecove. It had served as a base for her nursing services but the project had never developed into a fully-fledged hospital. The co-operative shop had, however, continued to trade right up to about 1945. Ó Concubhair said that she gifted equipment to the Nurses' Missionary League for use in their hospitals in India and sold the roof timber, slates and other materials. She presented the proceeds to the White Cross Fund, which supported the families of the many republican prisoners who were in the Curragh Camp at the time.

One of the most fascinating aspects of the story of this aristocrat, republican, nurse, champion of the poor, nurses' union firebrand, vegetarian and church organist was the legal battle her last will and testament provoked. In 1940 she willed all she owned 'for the benefit of the Republicans of the time according to the objects of the Republicans as they were in the years 1919 to 1921'. But, as Ó Concubhair explained, by the time she died, on 16 January 1955, it was very difficult to decide who these republicans might be and what the objects had been and so the whole matter ended up in the High Court in 1978–79. Mr Justice Gannon, one of three different judges to hear the case, ruled the will 'void for remoteness', despite such diverse bodies as the 1916–21 Club, Sinn Féin, the Workers' Party and the government claiming to be the rightful 'Republicans of the time'. The eventual beneficiary was her nephew, the Earl of Midleton. According to Stoakley, the value of Gobnait's estate had been very small at the time of her death but the court was told it had eventually risen to £17,000.

At her funeral in the village of Sneem, Gobnait Ní Bhruadair's coffin, wrapped in the Tricolour, was borne by John Joe Sheehy, Seán Ryan, Jer Riordan and John Joe Rice, all prominent republicans. In August 1968 a Celtic cross was unveiled over her grave by John Joe Sheehy. Of the thousands of tourists who pass through Sneem every summer, very few are aware of the fascinating life story of the Englishwoman who now sleeps under the Celtic cross in the peaceful churchyard near the narrow stone bridge.

The Eight-Foot Bed

Possibly the most politically significant 'tourist' to visit Kerry in the twentieth century was former French President Charles de Gaulle (1890–1970), a towering European states-man who led his country's opposition to the Nazis during the Second World War and founded the French Fifth Republic in 1958. His visit to Ireland on 10 May 1969 trained the eyes of the western world on Kerry.

Aged seventy-eight at the time, de Gaulle, with his wife Yvonne, flew into Cork Airport by French military jet. The village of Sneem, where the couple stayed in a small hotel called Heron Cove on the shores of Kenmare Bay, was suddenly thrust into the limelight. De Gaulle's unexpected resignation as French president on 28 April 1969 had caused uproar and he had come under pressure to declare which candidate would have his support in the ensuing election. Barely a fortnight after he stepped down from office, he decided to leave all the controversy behind and retreated to Ireland for a 'quiet holiday', which turned out to be anything but as the world's media descended on Kerry.

Among the contingent were the county's leading press reporters and photo journalists of the day: husband and wife team Pádraig and Joan Kennelly, who ran a news agency in Tralee, *Kerryman* editor Seamus McConville and photographers Kevin Coleman and Donal and Harry MacMonagle. As it turned out, the homegrown press was to scoop the international media in spectacular fashion.

On the morning the de Gaulles flew into Cork, Pádraig and Joan Kennelly had been due to fly out to Spain on holiday. Instead, the couple's travel plans were switched to a speedy drive to the gates of Heron Cove. With news of his views on the election in high demand, film crews from the US and Britain, including the BBC and ITV, were hot on his trail. About sixty journalists placed themselves in the Parknasilla Great Southern Hotel and even hired boats to try to film the de Gaulles from the sea; the gardaí also took to the sea to frustrate their efforts.

Pádraig Kennelly's prized shots were taken, however, from an upstairs window of Derrynane House, ancestral home of Daniel O'Connell. As a local, Pádraig was convinced that de Gaulle would visit Derrynane because it was the most important historical building in South Kerry and because O'Connell had been revered throughout Europe. The most valuable shot of the visit was, however, taken by Joan Kennelly, who was on the spot to capitalise on a very lucky break.

Joan had been a keen photographer from a young age and, as a young woman, she returned from Spain with a film of photographs of bullfighting, which she handed in to a local pharmacist to be developed. That pharmacist was Pádraig, who convinced her not to return to Spain and, shortly afterwards, to become his wife.

Joan was positioned among the congregation in the parish church at Sneem the morning the de Gaulles attended Sunday Mass. The French couple elected to sit in the body of the church among the locals – no special pew. When de Gaulle stood, in formal French Catholic style, at a point when the locals remained kneeling, Joan seized the opportunity to photograph him towering over the congregation. She was removed from the church by Special Branch detectives, who, amazingly, did not confiscate the camera. The exclusive rights to the image, *La Prière du générale*, or *The Prayer of the General*, were bought by the iconic French magazine *Paris Match*, and the negative was sent to Paris on the evening it was taken. 'It was the most valuable photo we ever marketed, and there was many a glass raised in the Kennelly household to General and Madame de Gaulle,' Pádraig said.

Kerryman editor Seamus McConville, a towering figure himself, fronted his paper on 17 May with the headline, 'Sneem Makes the World Headlines'. He compared the impact of the visit to that of the late President John F. Kennedy to Ireland six years before. His detailed report conveyed the impact of the visit locally. Sneem postmaster John Mangan said they had never handled as many calls on their switchboard. Calls were coming in at an average of 600 a day, twice the exchange's average. A week later a photo in *The Kerryman* featured General de Gaulle giving a smile and a salute to Mrs Kathleen Fitzgerald, Drimnaghbeg, Sneem, as he left Mass at the church in Sneem. 'Mrs Fitzgerald is a niece of Miss May McCarthy, who was visited by Madame de Gaulle in Kenmare Hospital the previous day,' the caption read. May McCarthy had been a governess to Madame de Gaulle's family in Calais when the Frenchwoman was only fourteen years old. Matron Mary Cronin said the two women had 'greeted each other like old friends'. McConville also reported that speculation that the de Gaulles were about to leave Sneem began when Kenmare barber Peter Hanley and Sneem hairdresser Peggy O'Sullivan were brought to the hotel on the Tuesday morning. The general had a trim and a shampoo and his wife a set.

Heron Cove, formerly a private residence, was leased at the time by an Englishman, Richard Stanford, who had flown with the Pathfinder Force of the Royal Air Force's Bomber Command over France during the Second World War. His lease ended the following September. *The Kerryman* reported that the place had been sold, along with 150 acres, to a member of the Cork firm Roches Stores. Just before the arrival of the couple on the Saturday, an eight-foot bed had been delivered for the former president. According to McConville, the bed was swapped for twin beds the following day because the general claimed that the mattress was too hard.

The de Gaulles moved from Sneem to Killarney on 3 June and stayed at Dairy Cottage, close to St Mary's cathedral, until 16 June. Here they had the 'quiet holiday' they had come to Ireland for. Dairy Cottage was then owned by Mrs Beatrice Grosvenor, a descendant of the earls of Kenmare. Her own home, Killarney House, was nearby. Mrs Grosvenor also owned the Castlerosse Hotel, which used Dairy Cottage as accommodation for guests.

Dairy Cottage is now in the Killarney National Park and has an interesting history. Designed by architect George Devey and completed between 1875 and 1878 as part of Killarney House, it was listed in early documents as 'Lady Kenmare's Dairy' and also as the 'Model Dairy'. As well as being a functioning dairy for the big house, it also served as a tea room for guests of the Kenmares and was linked by ornamental walks to the nearby mansion. Apparently many VIPs visited for afternoon tea, served in the front drawing room, which can be seen in pictures from the Lawrence Collection from *c.* 1890, showing oak panelling and a noteworthy collection of Wedgwood and toby jugs. The cottage was extensively altered and extended by Mrs Grosvenor towards the end of the 1950s. In 1972 it came into state ownership as part of the Knockreer estate, which had been owned by Mrs Grosvenor.

In early May 2011 I visited Pádraig Kennelly at his home in 22 Ashe Street, Tralee. He was lying on a sofa, obviously weakened from his long battle with cancer, but he was animated as he spoke about his upcoming journey to Paris. A selection of photos he and Joan had taken were to form an exhibition, *De Gaulle, A Quiet Holiday*. I thought he did not have the strength to travel. A week later, I opened his family newspaper, *Kerry's Eye*, to see him standing at the podium in the Centre Culturel Irlandais. That was Pádraig to the end, an original. Pádraig and Joan, who have since passed over, took some half a million photographs of Kerry life in their time, today archived at www.kennellyarchive.com.

Big Bertha

A s the cow ambled in the front door of the Blackwater Tavern, a little boy in the crowd was walking somewhat too close to the beast's nether quarters for his mother's liking. 'Brian, stand back in case she'd deposit,' she cautioned. This was no ordinary cow and this was no ordinary Monday morning in the rural bar, located between the village of Sneem and Moll's Gap. Big Bertha, the oldest cow in the world, had reached the ripe old age of forty-seven the previous day, 9 March 1992. She might have been toothless and geriatric, but Bertha had leapt into the *Guinness Book of Records* not only for her longevity but also for her lifetime breeding, with thirty-nine calves to her credit.

The Blackwater Tavern, Bertha's local, was heaving with humanity that Monday morning to celebrate bovinity elevated to celebrity status. Social assignments do not come any more glitzy for this journalist, who had been dispatched from Killarney to record the birthday celebrations of the speckled cow that had first gained a hoofhold in the national imagination in 1986. Even the national broadcaster had ventured outside the Pale to 'milk' the occasion. RTÉ's Joe Duffy, who was given the honour of hosting an outside broadcast for *The Gay Byrne Show* dedicated exclusively to the long-lived cow, was told all about 'milk music' – drumming the bottom of buckets during milking time. Music, song and storytelling with an elemental theme set the national airwaves crackling.

'The bull is nearly extinct,' Kenmare storyteller Nancy Price told Duffy. 'It's the man with the white collar and tie.'

'Did the cows miss the bull?' the Dub mused.

'Miss the bull?' Gay Byrne slagged him at the other end of the line. 'You daft eejit.'

Tralee singer Christie Hennessy serenaded Bertha, who leaned her head dreamily beside a creamy pint on the bar counter. Her owner, Jerome O'Leary, a bachelor farmer, stood beside her, beaming proudly.

While Jerome clearly enjoyed all the attention that came with Bertha's celebrity status, he had an innate sense of generosity that elevated the experience far beyond a publicity stunt. He teamed up with Donie Riney, Sneem, and Pat O'Connell, Killarney, each battling cancer, to raise more than £50,000 for Aid Cancer Treatment (ACT) through Bertha's public appearances. Leading out the St Patrick's Day Parade annually in Sneem was one of Bertha's biggest fund-raising 'gigs'. Jerome confessed to giving her whiskey beforehand to 'steady her nerves'. He maintained that her lively temperament had inspired his parents to call her after the infamous German gun, Big Bertha, after she was bought as a calf at the fair in Sneem on 17 March 1945.

The authenticity of Bertha's age was a question Jerome fielded with nonchalance; no need for expensive PR consultants to fend off the media. The proof hinged on the discovery of a special ear mark used for indicating TB testing long before ear tags were introduced, he explained. In addition to the discovery of this mark, there were the findings of a laboratory test carried out in Cork. 'One lad below there said no one will eat a bite of her – she's as yellow as a sovereign,' he stated. Most significantly, he attributed Bertha's longevity to her breeding. She came from the ancient Droimeann line of cattle, bred to survive on poor or mountainy land and characterised by speckled colouring and a white stripe running right along the back from the tail to the ears. The Gaelic form of the word, *Droimfhionn*, is derived from *droim* meaning 'ridge' and *fhionn* meaning 'pale' or 'white'.

References to this hardy breed go back over 1,000 years. Droimeann cattle are believed to have originated in the Near East and to have migrated across Europe to Ireland. In Kerry they are almost exclusively found in a triangle of countryside between Sneem, Kenmare and Glencar.

Bertha could have lived and died in obscurity but for Jerome's fondness for conversing about her with the owners of the Blackwater Tavern, Teddy and Mary O'Neill. Teddy got in touch with one of Kerry's weekly newspapers, the *Kingdom*, in 1986. Editor Harry MacMonagle and journalist John O'Mahony did not look a gift cow in the mouth, and a media sensation was born. Bertha's fame spread worldwide as two entries in the *Guinness Book of Records* followed.

The popularity of Bertha and the crusade to raise money for cancer treatment transformed the life of the rural bachelor beyond measure. With her passing on 31 December 1993, at the age of forty-eight, his horizons narrowed once again. Some years later, an emigrant uncle of mine, Pat Joy, was home on holidays from London with his partner, Eileen, and I took them around the Ring of Kerry. From Sneem we found our way to Jerome O'Leary's home at Geragh South. In the kitchen of the relatively modern bungalow, a shotgun lay across a worktop even more cluttered than my own. There was a black truncheon also with a retractable spike; rural isolation carries its own fear of intruders.

But the real purpose of our pilgrimage was in the hallway. The four of us stood there regarding Bertha, preserved for posterity through the art of taxidermy. To Jerome, she seemed no less a marvel in suspended animation than when she was dipping her speckled head lustily into a bucket of meal. 'Bertha' my uncle said, in a tone somewhere between delight and reverence. I deigned to enquire how one of her legs appeared to be balding. Jerome informed us that he had stationed her too close to a radiator and the leg had been singed.

Researching the fate of Bertha for this book, I learned that after Jerome himself had gone to his maker, she remained there on her own in the abandoned house for many years. There is something terribly lonesome about the image of the cow 'standing in state' on dark nights with mountain winds whistling around the cold house. Maybe it was Jerome's intervention from the heavenly pastures, but George Kelly, a farmer from Beaufort near Killarney, got in touch with some of his relatives, who were happy to entrust her to his care. The years in solitary confinement had taken their toll, but George had Bertha refurbished to bring up her natural speckled and 'burgundy' tones. Visitors to Hazelfort Farm between Killarney and Killorglin can view Big Bertha in her new resting place set against a backdrop of lowland pastures infinitely more fertile than the rushy fields she was reared in.

Her story is fittingly preserved in a series of framed photos and newspaper articles in the Blackwater Tavern where she took her first steps to media stardom. And, yes, that concerned mother proved correct back in 1992 at the birthday bash because Bertha did in fact make a deposit before she left the bar – an insignificant contribution in comparison to the impression she made on the county's imagination.

The Little Nest

It remains to be seen if the heritage plaques relating the history of Kenmare will feature an input on the late Margaret Thatcher any day soon, but the town does have a direct ancestral link to one of the most controversial political leaders to tread this planet. The Iron Lady's lineage can be traced back to the townland of Dromanassig, halfway between Bonane and Kenmare on the road to Bantry. Here, in a simple stone cottage three and a half miles from Kenmare, Maggie's great-grandmother, Catherine O'Sullivan, first saw the light of day in the early 1800s. She emigrated to Wales and moved from there to England, working as either a maid or a washerwoman depending on the degree to which you wish to embellish the tale. Little did Catherine imagine who was coming after her on a branch yet to sprout on the family tree, but maybe hard times had already forged some iron in her emigrant spirit.

The formidable prime minister's neglect of her Kenmare

ancestry was her loss, because Dromanassig is located in the wild splendour of the Sheen Valley where the Sheen river cascades down rock faces into gravel-bedded pools. The Gaelic, *An Drom*, the back, signifies a slight gradual slope. According to Monsignor Pádraig Ó Fiannachta, an *assaig* may contain the word *eas* or *easach*, which would mean 'of the many waterfalls'. But it could also come from the adjective *fás* meaning 'empty', and *fásach*, a noun very often used in placenames and meaning wasteland. He concluded, 'I have never come across "of the many waterfalls" in our placenames. I think vegetation and occupation were of great importance. Although *easach* translates as "of the many waterfalls" in Old Irish, the townland's name of Dromanassig most likely means "the place of the wasteland".'

There is surely work for a poetic imagination in the interpretation of the supposition that Margaret Thatcher's forebears fled a 'wasteland'. But, who knows, the charm of the tumbling Sheen and of Kenmare might even have worked its way into Maggie's affections as it has done with countless visitors, including the Cork singer-songwriter Jimmy McCarthy, whose song 'Néidín' conveys how this little town with 'rhododendrons in her hair' nestles in people's hearts:

As I leave behind Néidín,
It's like purple splashed on green,
My soul is strangely fed,
Through the winding hills ahead,
And she plays a melody,
On wind and streams for me,
Won't you remember,

Won't you remember,

Won't you remember me?

Jimmy drew on the town's Irish name, which translates as the 'little nest'. The old Gaelic name for the town is *Ceann Mhara*, the head of the sea.

Two corners of Kenmare are my firm favourites: Parnell Place and Rock Street, with its sloping line of quaint old dwelling houses and, at the top end, an ivy-topped stone wall running east to west. Townsman Bobby Hanley, who is sharing his local knowledge, tells me that this wall segment is the remnants of an extensive stone wall that once encircled the Lodge Wood. At the top of the wood stood Lansdowne Lodge, residence of the agent of the Lansdowne landlord family, who owned a vast estate in the area. Halfway down the laneway, edged with the remains of shanty houses, the stonework near the base of the wall changes where a hole has been filled in. Back in the 1940s the hole in the wall was a gateway into another world for Bobby Hanley and his friends, who scrambled through it and into the cover of the old trees where the imagination had no limits.

The remains of the tiny house opposite the former hole in the wall was once the home of a Mrs Harrington, whose husband was killed in the First World War. Her son, an emigrant, told Bobby a story from the era of the Black and Tans. An Irish Volunteer, who was on the run after the Headford Ambush of 21 March 1921 at a railway station near Killarney, fled to the house of Mrs Harrington and her family. 'She got the brainwave of telling him to get up on the wall and to lie in the ivy when the Black and Tans were searching,' Bobby related. The man evaded capture.

At the opposite end of the wall, a picturesque terrace of houses runs in the direction of the steeple of Holy Cross church. Below the end house, where a woodsman used to live, the ground falls away to a cut-stone building which was formerly the office for the land agent of the landlord family, the Lansdownes. This building, overlooking the triangular green in the town square, has a bricked-up gable window. Local legend has it that the agent, William Steuart Trench (1808–72), opposed the building of the Catholic church by Archdeacon John O'Sullivan and closed the window up so that he would not have to look at it. Fr O'Sullivan allegedly vowed that he would 'crow over' Trench, hence the cockerel weather vane on the church steeple. Bobby is dubious about this story and believes that the two men co-operated with each other.

At the top of Rock Street, there is an inscription, 'Victoria Terrace, 1871', on one of the houses beside the wall. Bobby recalls that a tailor, Charlie Golden, lived in the corner house. Rock Street was home to another family of tailors, the Leahy Brothers, one of whom was a well-known poet in the town. The street also has a proud tradition when it comes to sport, as Bobby explains: 'A hurling team came out of this street alone; they had their own fifteen in the 1920s. There was very little football played in Kenmare then – it was a foreign game and new in the scheme of things. Kenmare won the Kerry County Hurling Championship in 1889.'

At the top of the street, there is a break in the wall allowing pedestrians to pass through. On the left, a stone tower,

Hutchinson's Folly, rises out of the trees. The structure is believed to have been named after an American who came to Kenmare in the 1800s, who built it to honour the soldiers who fought in the battle of Bunker Hill in June 1775, part of the American War of Independence. Close by, at the other side of the housing estate, is a wide entrance directly in line with that of Kenmare Golf Club. From here, Bobby explains, the driveway to the old lodge swept to the left and curved round again. The lodge, which was still habitable up to the mid-1970s, was used as an overflow for the Lansdowne Hotel.

Bobby remembers one particular guest, the English composer Ernest Jack Moeran (1894–1950), who arrived in Kenmare from Valentia Island some time in the 1930s on a bus run by the Whartons, a local family. 'There were a few nice rooms on top. Jack Moeran had a piano in one of them. I remember he was supposed to go to Norwich for a music festival. He said, "How can you leave Kenmare on a morning like this?"'

Moeran, whose compositions were influenced by folk music, mixed very well with the locals and was a regular in the billiards room in the Lansdowne Arms. 'What did you compose today, Leahy, walking down here?' he once enquired of the poet from Rock Street. Bobby, who is a great admirer of the composer's music, used to be proprietor of the Lansdowne and christened it 'Moeran's Bar' in his memory. Sadly, as in the case of many creative spirits, alcohol took over Moeran's life and he died at a comparatively young age. He now lies in the old Church of Ireland graveyard on the Kilgarvan Road under the epitaph, 'He rests in the mountain country which he loved so well.'

We walk through the entrance of Kenmare Golf Club,

founded in 1903, and continue beyond the colonial-style wooden clubhouse on the route that the Lansdowne agent took to Sunday service in St Patrick's Church of Ireland church on Bell Heights, alternatively called the Sound, which is the old name that Bobby favours. As we walk, Bobby relates how the Lansdowne family, also known as the earls of Shelburne, once owned St Stephen's Green in Dublin, and their town house, Kerry House, was located close to where the Shelbourne Hotel stands today. The story goes that when the Lansdownes refused permission for the Shelburne name to be used for the hotel in 1849, the purchaser, Martin Burke, got round the impasse by adding an 'o'.

At the other side of the car park, once called Mahony's Height, the right of way continues through a break in the boundary wall with the Park Hotel, previously a Great Southern Hotel and dating from 1897. The terraced lawns sweeping down towards Kenmare Bay were once entirely devoted to a vegetable garden. There is an option here of walking down through the woods to the edge of the bay and turning left towards the boathouse and taking a right to continue on the Renagross Walk. Outside the hotel gates, we take a left along Shelburne Street, past the Lime Tree Restaurant, which was once the Protestant school. The building to its right was the teacher's residence. In the late 1940s the school became a co-educational secondary school with a 'bohemian spirit'. Across the street, the building beside the disused petrol pumps was the bridewell, one of Kenmare's oldest buildings.

At the end of Shelburne Street, we take a left to visit the hilltop St Patrick's church, which is full of history. There is a wall plaque 'in affectionate memory' of George Mahony Mayberry, MD, JP, Riversdale, Kenmare, who died on 12 June 1880, aged eighty, and 'who tended the sick and dying throughout the years of famine and distress'. But this is a church that moves with the times; it has a crèche-like facility with children's books and toys.

Muxnaw Mountain, rising in the south-east, dominates this side of the town and, as Bobby explains, it is woven into everyday conversation, often in terms of predicting the weather. For instance, 'I can't see Muxnaw today.' The view down Henry Street, with all its colourful shopfronts, to the copper-plated church spire is the stuff of postcards. It was named after the 3rd Marquis of Lansdowne, Henry Petty-Fitzmaurice (1780–1863). Bobby grew up in No. 17.

Further down the street is the Marble Arch, at the opening of which used to stand a bar called 'Lizzie Flynn's Old Saloon'. It had an enormous backyard from where she sold milk and where the 'stud horse' operated on fair days. At the back of the laneway was a series of tiny houses that earned the nickname 'China Town' because people lived in such cramped conditions.

We turn onto New Road to discover rows of old-style cottages, beginning with the picturesque Parnell Place and leading onto Pound Lane, the location of the animal pound. We can still see traces of workplaces of Kenmare tradesmen long passed: the three blacksmiths, Michael Cronin, Jimmy Creedon, the Smith Harrington, and the town carter, Jerry Sheehan. Pound Lane became Emmett Place in the early 1900s; Davitt's Place is nearby. Around here lived the three Healy brothers, who were nicknamed Thunder, Lightning and

Calm. Mike, alias 'Thundering Mike', became a familiar figure in Killarney from the 1960s onwards, but he moved between the two towns.

On Market Street, where the houses are beautiful, though several are derelict, we turn left for the ancient Kenmare stone circle. A limestone outcrop protrudes from the final terrace of tiny houses. This is part of a limestone seam running east from Kilgarvan, along the banks of the Roughty river, through Kenmare and out to sea. The very first house on Market Street, an end house with a limestone outcrop in the garden beside it, was the home of a local poet, Tom Lovett. At the far end of the street near the square, we note the date, 1874, and the letter L for Lansdowne over one of the doors.

The triangular green in the centre of the square and the streets converging in an X shape are all part of the town plan drawn up by William Rowell, a grandson of Sir William Petty. Petty had been granted the entire Kenmare area by Oliver Cromwell as part payment for completing the mapping of Ireland in the Down Survey of 1656. He laid out the modern town c. 1670.

Entering the square, Market House, built in the 1880s, is on the right. In its vicinity are Rose Cottage, home to the Poor Clare sisters and the famous 'Nun of Kenmare', Sister Mary Frances Cusack, in the 1860s; the little footbridge called Cromwell's Bridge; near it, Our Lady's Well; and Holy Cross church, where you mustn't forget to look up and see the fourteen angels carved from Bavarian pine. Incidentally, Oliver Cromwell never visited Kenmare. One explanation for Cromwell's Bridge is that it is shaped like a moustache, which is a *croimeal* in Irish. Another footbridge hidden away at the back of the car park opposite

Holy Cross church is a real curiosity in its construction and its antiquity, and is worth seeking out, even though it is closed off by a locked gate in the centre because it now leads into private property.

One of the Kenmare personalities recalled by Bobby is Bessie 'Carraig' O'Sullivan, who had a tiny shop at No. 35 Main Street. Bessie celebrated her hundredth birthday in 1975, though some people would say she was older than that. One of Bessie's memories furnished a living link to the original Catholic church that was replaced at the head of Main Street by the bank building. 'Her brother used to play handball against the remaining gable of the church,' Bobby said. 'She was the last person in this town to recall anything like that.'

Down at the pier at the edge of the town, there is a concrete road laid down in the 1960s by a German man, the promoter of a 'buttons and bows' factory that never materialised. At the end of the road is Sonny Palmer's Field. Here, in a simple four-post hayshed, Jack Moeran, on the dry but destitute, spent his final days. On 1 December 1950 his body was washed up on the shore at Roger's Beach near the pier. His inquest suggested that he had died before he entered the water and that his death was accidental. Bobby feels that a stormy south-western wind blew him off the pier. 'Others said he left himself go. It could be a mixture of the two. No one knows.'

Rinuccini Road

The sights on the byroad leading to Ardea on the edge of Kenmare Bay are no more remarkable than those on any other Kerry byroad: a national school, fuchsia hedges, a scattering of holiday homes between farmhouses and the sea pounding the shore at the road's end. To get there, follow the Castletownbere Road from Kenmare for about three miles and take a right turn into the narrow road, known locally as the High Road, where the national school, *Réalt na Mara*, Star of the Sea, is set at its very beginning.

This road, where Tuosist Post Office is also a marker, sees little enough traffic today, but turn the clock back almost 400 years and picture how remote Ardea Castle and its coastal community must have been. Imagine then the wonder induced by the appearance on 22 October 1645 of a foreign frigate sailing in from the open sea with a gilded figurehead of St Peter at the prow. Among the tanned strangers who came ashore in a small boat was Papal Nuncio Extraordinary, John Baptist Rinuccini, who was bound for Kilkenny on a diplomatic mission. (For this reason I have christened the High Road 'Rinuccini Road'.)

But why had the *San Pietro* anchored in Kenmare Bay so far from Rinuccini's destination? T. J. Barrington explains that the frigate, which had sailed from France, had been hotly pursued by a 'renegade Irishman', Plunkett, with two vessels of the parliament squadron, until a fire broke out in the galley of his own ship. The fire gave an advantage to the cardinal's ship, which had slipped into Kenmare Bay to evade its pursuers. The eminent cardinal, who was also archbishop of Fermo, had been sent to Ireland by Pope Innocent X on a mission to unite the old Irish Catholics and the Anglo-Irish Catholics at a summit-style gathering called the Confederation of Kilkenny.

Accustomed undoubtedly to lavish apartments in Italy, the cardinal spent his first night in Ireland in a shepherd's hut in Ardea. In a diary written by one of his retinue, there is an account of their arrival 'al porto di Kilmar' and of the warm reception and the courtesy of the poor, who impressed the visitors also with the depth of their religious faith.

Why the cardinal did not stay in Ardea Castle is not clear. Historian Gerard Lyne, who has retired from the National Library to his native Lauragh, near Kenmare, said that the head of the Ardea family in 1641 was Ellen O'Sullivan, a widow who had been married to the eldest son of Philip of Ardea, tánaiste (leader) to Sir Owen O'Sullivan Beare. *The Books of Survey and Distribution* show her forfeiting several townlands round Ardea Castle in 1641. Colonel Donogh Mac Fínín (McCarthy) had become the owner of the castle; he was also proprietor of Ardtully Castle, where Rinuccini was later received. 'It may be that the widow had been in financial difficulties after her husband's death and had disposed of the castle,' he said. Today the ruined Ardea Castle stands on the private land of the Lansdowne estate and is entirely obliterated by undergrowth. For generations, all the houses in the locality were built facing the castle.

Having spent two days in Ardea, the cardinal proceeded to

Kilgarvan where he spent two nights at Ardtully Castle before heading to Limerick and, eventually, Kilkenny. His ship, which was carrying a large consignment of arms and money, went to Dingle, from where the arms were landed and transferred to Limerick.

A slip road beside Tuosist Post Office connects the High Road to the Coast Road on which is set the Parish Hall, which is still in the townland of Ardea. A plaque on the hall façade commemorates the folklorist Seán Ó Súilleabháin (1903–96), whose birthplace was Derrylough, Tuosist. His parents were teachers at Leithead National School. Having trained as a teacher, Ó Súilleabháin joined the Irish Folklore Commission in 1935 and was instrumental in setting up the Schools' Folklore Scheme three years later.

Beyond Ardea, the drive that continues along the coast to Kilmackillogue is, for my money, among the most scenic drives in the world for the expanse of sea and sky and the rugged landscape; the bonus is that you will hardly meet a soul along the way. Across the bay is the Parknasilla Hotel, where the writer, George Bernard Shaw, stayed in Room 3 in 1909. He crossed by boat to Kilmackillogue, where the local tailor, Michael O'Sullivan, measured him for tweed suits that were later posted to London. Another famous visitor, this time in the early years of the twenty-first century, was Caroline Kennedy, who dropped into Helen Moriarty's Bar and Guest House beside Kilmackillogue Pier. If the day is fine, one could do worse than sit on the little fishing pier across the road from the bar, previously O'Sullivan's, and enjoy a Guinness and a bowl of steamed mussels with brown soda bread as I have done on a cycling trip in the past. This circular route from Kenmare makes a wonderful cycle of about thirty miles – for the fit.

Continuing inland from Kilmackillogue, the wooded road leads past Derreen House and Gardens, which are part of the Lansdowne estate. Development of the semi-tropical gardens, nurtured by the Gulf Stream, was begun in 1870 by the 5th Marquis, Henry Petty-Fitzmaurice. In his time as Viceroy of India and Governor of Canada he brought many species back to Derreen. Southern hemisphere tree ferns, which only grow under glass in Dublin, flourish here. The gardens, which have a real wilderness feel despite their many exotic shrubs, are open to the public in season.

From Derreen we rejoin the main road to Castletownbere at Lauragh and turn left towards Kenmare. If you have time, especially if you are a hillwalker, take the immediate right past the former Síbin Bar, where one Sunday afternoon I sat in on an unforgettable ballroom-dancing session. The narrow cul-de-sac road leads into the valley of Cummeengeara, once home to Cornelius Sullivan Reagh, who was hanged in Tralee in 1831, having been found guilty of the murder of his aunt seventeen years before.

The fate of Sullivan, who was known as *Rábhach*, has entered local folklore; the valley is also known as Rábhach's Glen. A report on his hanging, published in the *Kerry Evening Post* on 23 March 1831, stated, 'On the scaffold he appeared quite collected, a very few convulsive struggles marked his exit from the world.' A sad footnote to the story is that his elderly father travelled to Tralee on horseback to bring home his son's clothes. This detail would tally with the old custom of attaching particular significance to the clothes of the dead. For instance, when a person died, a friend would wear the dead person's clothes for three Sundays so that the deceased would have them in the next world.

Different versions of the valley's story have been woven down through the years, with other victims being substituted for the aunt in some cases. A comprehensive study of the many versions was published in 2012 by Janet Murphy, who quotes a passage from the English writer James Anthony Froude (1818–94), author of *A Fortnight in Kerry*, who had leased Derreen in the 1860s. In Froude's account, which was published in *Fraser's Magazine*, a sailor jumped ship in Castletownbere with a bag of sovereigns and crossed the mountains to Cummeengeara. He found shelter in the home of a farmer, referred to as O'Brien by Froude. The farmer, overcome with greed, murdered the sailor for the gold. A servant girl called Kathleen witnessed the murder from a loft above but held her counsel. When she eventually blurted out her secret in anger to the farmer, he murdered her by flinging her over a waterfall. Years later, his crime was revealed by a secret witness who had been on the mountain that day.

On a remote site, about 320 metres above the Glenstrastel Valley, is a prized example of ancient rock engravings, *Carraig na Scríob*. It is also referred to as *Pluais na Scríob*, the Cave of the Writings. The structure consists of a large sandstone slab rock leaning on a sandstone boulder, creating a kind of tunnel or cave. The engravings are found on the boulder face in the shadow of the sheltering slab. Despite several examinations by archaeologists, the meaning of the engravings remains an enigma. There is speculation that they date back to the Stone

Age or to the Bronze Age. I walked up there many years ago with a group from Tuosist on a day fit to float the Ark, and I can tell you it is far from a saunter. If you would like to see the rock, I would recommend hiring a local guide.

On the journey back to Kenmare is Dawros church, which is very popular for weddings and which was built in about 1875 by a Lixnaw priest, Fr John Barton, from his own finances on land donated by the Lansdowne estate. Shortly after the church was built, Fr Barton contracted typhoid while on a sick call to Ardea and died.

Lily of the Valley

L ily van Oost came down the road with a black and white dog in her arms, a neighbour by her side and a worried look on her face. The neighbour had found Bran, the dog, thrown by the roadside and badly bitten. Lily concluded that he had been attacked by a fox and, given the location of the wounds, that he stood a good chance of taking a case for indecent assault. That was a sunny August afternoon in 1986, and I had driven through the Gap of Dunloe in search of the Flemish artist who had left behind the crowded city of Antwerp to respond to her muse in the wild and lonely splendour of Kerry's famous Black Valley, becoming known as Lily of the Valley in the process.

While she waited for water to boil to treat Bran's wounds, Lily delivered snatches of her life story and, at intervals, shooed bantam hens and clutches of chickens from the porch door. 'The bloody hens are screaming my head off,' she said in exasperation. On both sides of the garden path banks of flowers were blazing. Lemon edged the peachy trumpets of a flower she called 'Granny's Bonnet'. Waves of blue, red, green and purple all combined to present a startling oasis of colour floating among the muted tones of the Kerry landscape.

Lily adored her garden. With a botanist's zeal and a mother's tender touch, she pointed out the various species and reeled off Latin names effortlessly. Ironically, one of the few plants she had not succeeded in coaxing out of the soil of her mountain garden was Lily of the Valley. Her blend of fertiliser was unique: wool, chicken dung and the heads of sheep and cows. 'Under the fruit trees I have the skull of a cow decomposing. All the juices go into the ground – the best fertiliser you can get. I use the skulls for sculptures going to the [Guinness] Hop Store.'

Like her garden, Lily must have been a startling apparition when she swept into the valley that first day, with her fearsome energy, dramatic pronouncements and wildly expressive eyes that missed nothing. She was an opera in herself, larger than life and always striving to be at the heart of life. 'I want them to gossip about me,' she told me. 'It keeps them happy. I bought a new bed last week, and my neighbours wanted to know was it a double or a single. I told them it takes three.'

Born in 1933, she was fiercely proud of her Flemish origins and later admonished me for referring to her as 'Belgian'. With the first money she ever earned in Belgium, she bought a box of pastels and a loom. She told me this as Bran was doused with water laced with Domestos (vodka having been considered but ruled out). She enrolled in art school in Antwerp, emerging five years later with a master's in Fine Arts. She specialised in graphic art, painting and monumental fibre art.

After she moved to the Black Valley in the 1970s, the former Pretty Polly hosiery factory in Killarney supplied her with bales of coloured nylon for her work. She liked to 'torture' the fibres. On the day of our interview, she was preparing a work for an exhibition at the Guinness Hop Store in Dublin. She was depicting the future as the 'Age of Nylon', where the resources of the world were polluted and prostituted. Another piece, *Episcopate Obstetrics*, dealt with the interference of the church in women's affairs. Two years after my visit, when the powers that be grew nervous about her plans to knit a jumper for a Dublin bus as part of a major sculptors' conference, Lily turned her attention to the Ha'penny Bridge instead; this installation came to pass.

Bran was washed and rinsed and returned to his box none the worse for his bleaching. A wire-haired terrier with a sphinx-like calm, he remained unperturbed by the vagaries of his owner or his journeys down the winding valley road in the passenger seat of her blue van. A highly educated woman with an insatiable intellect, Lily may have withdrawn to the valley, but she never shut out the world. She was passionate about the cruelties of mankind. Cruelty and injustice inspired many of the themes of her art. A lot of her ideas came when she was so tired from work that her body was almost completely annihilated and her mind took over.

The poet Grace Wells came to live with Lily in the valley during the wet winter of 1991 with a view to ghostwriting her autobiography. It was the serendipity of seeing a wool coat made by Lily and worn by a stranger on a London street that inspired Grace to seek the artist out. In a radio essay for the RTÉ programme, *Sunday Miscellany*, she describes that inspiring coat as 'no ordinary coat, but a piece of living sculpture, woven and knitted and crocheted by Lily van Oost deep in the Kerry hills'. The essay continued on this theme:

> She had used raw wool, carded it and spun it, and taken up knitting needles and a crochet hook to create spiders' webs, dreadlocks, three-dimensional appendages that might have been mountains or running water or human forms. Into the fabric of that coat she sewed the bleat of sheep, and the sound of the wind blown over black lakes. The coat held the spirit of a place, and captured an indefinable spirit of art that I reached toward, longed for.

The poet arrived at Lily's door in October, and by the time she was ready to leave in April, the valley was 'filled with new light, the russet bracken glowed red' and 'leaves opened on the birches'. In collaboration with Lily, she had 'clocked up' 80,000 words. The fact that the life story was never ultimately published was beside the point, as Grace concluded in her radio piece:

> I've come to realise that twenty years ago there must have been a moment when that London stranger stood at the door of his house, deciding which jacket or coat to wear, his hand passing over denim and leather and nylon. What sorcery leapt from Lily's wool? Had

he made a different choice, everything of my life would have been unwound. I doubt I would have come to Ireland, or met Lily, or learned how spells are woven into the things we make, our crafts having their own lives, working their own magic, long after they leave our hands.

Lily's art was all-consuming. She described her appetite for work as her 'unlaziness'. Did she ever relax? 'No, no,' she replied, aghast. 'I sleep if I find the time. I am happy with almost nothing. If I have inspiration, I am the happiest woman in the world.' She described herself as a 'bit of a visionary'. To illustrate this, she delivered an anecdote about reading palms at a party in the Sneem holiday home of the late Dermot Kinlen, a barrister who went on to become a High Court judge. With the benefit of hindsight, she may have had even greater visionary powers than she suspected:

> I looked at one man's palm and said, 'Oh money, money, money.' I did not want to see that. Everyone was laughing. They thought I was a cheat because he was a director from the Bank of Ireland. I thought he was a cheat because he did not know people I knew from the Bank of Ireland in Dublin.

Lily was very particular as to the name for the extension she had built to house her looms and materials, and she took the pen from my hand to write the word 'atelier'. It was not a workshop or a studio, she emphasised. 'On the Continent, a studio is where a fancy man goes with his woman from two to four in the afternoon for the lovemaking thing,' she explained.

Her work features in museum of modern art collections in Brussels, Antwerp, Baghdad and Dublin. The Royal Albertina Library in Brussels acquired some twenty of her drawings. She also participated in an international exhibition organised by the 'Physicians against Nuclear War' to tour the capital cities of the world.

Lily lived a frugal, Spartan lifestyle, but what she had she shared generously. She was a woman of her word. 'I never promise something without having the intention of keeping my promise,' she said. 'I think it's ugly if you don't.' She walked me to the car that August day, apologising for not making tea, though she had served glasses of advocaat made from the bantams' eggs. She had no tea, and, anyway, making tea made her nervous.

Let the hands of the clock race forward to 1997, and a dark, cold October evening in Tralee. I had left the newspaper office and was dithering about driving straight home or calling into Kerry General Hospital to visit Lily. A candle burned on the window sill of her private room. It was lighting for a neighbour who was unwell. She was very little changed from the old self I had delighted in meeting down through the intervening years. The humour and the spirit were invincible, but a shadow darkened her countenance when she spoke of her breast cancer as a 'terrible thing'. She brightened when speaking of her daughters, Cathy and Nicky, who had visited her at Cork Regional Hospital before she had been transferred back to Kerry a few weeks before. Before I left, I stood at the end of the bed, teased her about her sense of mischief and promised to call to the valley during my November holidays.

Lily died peacefully in her sleep with her daughters at her bedside just a few weeks short of her birthday that November. She did not want a funeral. She directed that her body be donated to the Medical Faculty of University College Cork for research. She left her daughters a detailed set of instructions, right down to the most minute details, including which three plants they should give to a member of the hospital cleaning staff. She also made provisions for a 'Farewell Party' to be held in her valley home in celebration of her life. And, on that bleak evening, when the mountain streams foamed white down the black rock faces, we remembered with affection the generous, creative, mischievous, unlazy spirit of Lily of the Valley.

Mrs Herbert's Lovers

I n 1781, at the age of nineteen, Elizabeth Germain left her ancestral home in England to begin married life with her husband, Henry Arthur Herbert (1756–1821). He was six years her senior and had inherited Muckross House and estate from his father two years before. Just ten years after the society wedding, on 20 April 1791, *The Times* of London reported the elopement of Elizabeth with a Major Duff from Scotland. Herbert subsequently filed for divorce.

What drove the 'bewitching beauty' to bolt from her

cosseted life among the landed gentry of Kerry, abandoning her children in the process? Did Mrs Herbert, daughter of George, 1st Viscount Sackville, feel that the rain-laden skies of Muckross were bearing down on her? Was her barrister husband a kindly but boring man? While the answers to these questions will never amount to anything more than conjecture, a detailed contemporary account paints a picture of Elizabeth Germain as a strikingly beautiful young woman in possession of a flirtatious, carefree spirit – a spirit too free, perhaps, to be contained within the walls of a draughty Irish mansion.

A colourful pen portrait of the woman who was mistress of Muckross House was recorded by Dorothea Herbert, whose father, a Herbert of Muckross, served as a rector in County Tipperary. Her book, *Retrospections of an Outcast*, in which Mrs Herbert's flirtations and eventual elopement are chronicled, was published posthumously in 1929. Writing in 1785, four years after Henry and Elizabeth were married, she mentions a week-long visit from 'Mr Henry Herbert of Muckross who brought over his young wife for the first time from England'. She goes on to deliver this effusive description of the new Mrs Herbert:

> Of all the bewitching beauties I ever beheld she was the most fascinating, though some did not think her so handsome on account of her skin which was quite like an East Indian's: but for my part I was quite charmed. Her beautiful black eyes and eyebrows under a handsome forehead her long dark eyelashes and ebony hair, which fell in thick tresses below her waist, rendered her irresistible. Her mouth, her smile, her dimples were enchanting. Her skin was the

clearest brown. Her legs, arms, and whole person exquisitely turned, and her melodious voice would have melted the most frozen apathy.

According to Dorothea, Elizabeth had yet to visit Muckross. This may be explained by the fact that her husband had spent much of his early life in England where he had been educated and where he had qualified as a barrister. It can be surmised that when the young couple eventually moved to Muckross, the new wife must have found Kerry very different and remote from her previous life in England.

In one domestic episode recorded by Dorothea she comes across as a woman living at one remove from the life around her. The writer, on a family visit to Muckross House, observed that Elizabeth left the drawing room ostensibly to see if the beds were well aired for the visitors but remained in the nursery playing with the children; the result was that the guests saw little of her. Well, some of the guests, that is. A wild, carefree streak emerges in Dorothea's revelation that the young wife preferred racing on the lawn with the writer's brothers or with any gentlemen who dropped in.

But there were more sensational revelations to follow, as it emerged that Mrs Herbert got into a 'strong flirtation' with a Captain Baird. Discretion did not appear to be her strongest suit but, according to Dorothea, 'her playful wildness and innocent appearance would have tranquillised the most jealous-pated wretch into security'. Captain Baird appears to have been one in a string of dalliances.

How far some of the flirtations were carried is another question, but trysts in the hallowed ruins of Muckross Abbey between the lady of the house and one of the visiting gentlemen were eventually to land her in hot water. Given that the visitor in question, Captain Hedges of Macroom, was a relative of the Herberts, the feisty lady could have claimed she was at least 'keeping it in the family'. Dorothea leans towards tolerance rather than condemnation: 'She bewitched every heart and was equally bewitched by our cousin, Captain Hedges, then a visitant at Muckross.' There were no secrets in the close confines of Muckross, and the 'beautiful mistress was soon much-talked of with him and the Abbey mentioned as the place of rendez-vous'.

All this must have proved too trying for the patience of the long-suffering Henry, who dispatched his wayward wife to England, where her father locked her up for 'some time' and fed her on bread and water. Out of love for his wandering wife or concern for their children, Henry took her back again after she completed her 'rigid penance'.

Maybe she could see no alternative other than married life in Muckross, or maybe she genuinely recognised her husband as a good man and tried to do her best by him and the children. Dorothea relates that the couple lived for some time after on 'good terms' and had a daughter and two sons 'nearly as beautiful as their mother'. But the period of domestic harmony proved tragically transitory. According to archaeologist Patricia O'Hare, who heads up the research library at Muckross House, Henry Sackville Herbert, the eldest son of Henry and Elizabeth, died as a young child in a fire at Muckross, sometime in the mid-1780s. The trauma of the little boy's death appears to have sundered the family's fragile stability once again.

Historian and author Sinead McCoole writes that Henry Herbert had lived between England and Ireland while pursuing a political career. He represented East Grinstead, Sussex, from 1782 until his resignation in 1786. She surmises that his resignation may have been the cause of marital difficulties, because his wife continued to have flirtations. Dorothea Herbert writes that Mrs Herbert's restless mind could not content itself as mistress of that 'Elysium and all its delights' and, after various other 'imprudences', she eloped with Major Duff, leaving behind her children – the eldest, Bessy, who was nine years old and Charles, who was just six.

Curiouser and curiouser the tale of infidelity grows at this stage. The two star-crossed lovers took flight to the Continent as Henry sued for divorce. There Duff suffered a paralytic complaint which deprived him of the use of his limbs. Dorothea writes, 'And his faithful partner carried him up and down stairs on her back, so the story goes.' After Mr Herbert lost his wife and 'she her character', every newspaper 'echoed' their misfortunes. Here, the trail goes cold and there are no correspondents of the ilk of the observant Dorothea Herbert to let us know what kind of a life Elizabeth had, where she settled and when she died. She is said to have spent her final years on the Continent with the man she had forsaken her husband and children for.

Henry later married Frances Ring, whom he extolled for her 'rare attentions and uniform kindness' and of whom he said he never felt he could repay 'her fidelity'. He died at his London home in Little Smith Street in Westminster in 1821.

Doomed Mansion

I n its heyday, Killarney House must have seemed like the
Buckingham Palace of Killarney, but today, apart from local-
history enthusiasts, few people realise the absolute splendour of
the doomed mansion that stood on the heights of Knockreer.
Echoes of its grandeur have survived down through the years
in local references to 'the Mansion', which has practically
disappeared without trace.

A palatial red-brick structure, with myriad gables and oriels
set above themed terraced gardens, it commanded a panorama of
lake and mountain for a radius of about 15 miles. Construction
of the Elizabethan revival manor was begun in 1873 by the earls
of Kenmare, the Catholic ascendancy family who then lived in
Killarney but who had taken their title from Kenmare Castle,
their property in Hospital, County Limerick. The house was
one of the great wonders of nineteenth-century Kerry. In April
1885 the Prince of Wales, Albert Edward, later to become King
Edward VII, his wife Alexandra and his son Victor were guests
there. In 1897 they were followed by the Duke and Duchess
of York, later King George VI and Queen Mary. At the height
of its splendour, when the British royals were tripping up and
down the opulent marble staircase, few could have guessed that
the hilltop seat of the earls of Kenmare would have a lifespan of
barely forty years.

Lady Kenmare is credited with the desire to build the new

Z-shaped house, which was designed by the British architect George Devey (1820–86), assisted by W. H. Lynn of Belfast. Before the construction of the new house, in a section of their estate opposite St Mary's cathedral, Lord and Lady Kenmare, Valentine Augustus and Gertrude Browne, lived in Kenmare House, which was built in 1726 and which stood opposite the Munster Fusiliers monument and behind the current jarvey rank close to the town centre. Kenmare House was eventually demolished, but its stable block was preserved and eventually became the current Killarney House, which is due to open as a visitor and interpretative centre in 2015.

The location of the new house is said to have been suggested by Queen Victoria during her visit to Killarney in 1861. On Monday 26 August, Queen Victoria, accompanied by Albert, the Prince Consort, the Prince of Wales, Prince Alfred, Princess Alice and Princess Helena, stayed in Kenmare House with the Brownes; the royal party spent the following two nights in Muckross House as guests of the Herberts.

By the end of the 1870s over £100,000 had been spent on the expensive 'gingerbread house' (a caustic reference to the red-brick), which was lavishly decorated with marble and European works of art. But the Kenmares were to meet a financial fate similar to that of overambitious property owners and developers in the backwash of the 'Celtic Tiger' of the early twenty-first century. The expenditure on the house and the demesne, combined with the Land Wars, saw the aristocrats heavily mortgaged to the Scottish Standard Life Assurance Company. By 1882 the earl owed £227,000, which was not a surprising state of affairs, given the prodigal expenditure on the house contents. Kathleen O'Rourke describes this as follows in her book, *Old Killarney:*

> The door handles were fashioned from antique gold and silver watch-cases, the dining-room hangings were made of stamped Cordova leather, and most of the articles in the house were priceless objets d'art. Egyptian onyx was used for the altar and reredos in the lovely chapel; the candlesticks were made of silver-encrusted coral, and old Italian embroidery beautified the church vestments.

In the Parnell Commission, the watch-cases were said by Maurice Leonard, Land Agent to Lord Kenmare, to have been picked up throughout Europe for the purpose of decorating the mansion.

British Prime Minister William Gladstone defended Lord Kenmare in 1881, when conditions on the Killarney estate were discussed in the House of Commons. The building of the expensive house on the estate met with some resentment locally, and was considered a 'foolish and Quixotic idea' by the *Kerry Evening Post* on 8 June 1881. The Kerry politician T. M. Healy asked the following question (among much more vitriol) during a House of Commons debate on legislation dealing with Ireland on 24 March 1887:

> Why is it that at the present time your legislation is directed to the suppression of outrage? It is because Lord Kenmare has insisted on building his great mansion there, and on having for handles to his doors the backs of Louis Quatorze watches; while in the surrounding neighbourhood are dwellings for the people as miserable as any huts

human beings could possibly live in. It is because, cheek by jowl with Lord Kenmare's magnificent castle, adorned and equipped with all the luxuries and artistic embellishments that wealth can procure, are the miserable pigsties of the men Lord Kenmare and his crowd have been robbing for years.

According to the Kenmare Papers, the Kenmare estates were the scene of a series of bitter struggles between 1880 and 1890, a decade in which Lord Kenmare was actually bankrupt. At one point, twenty-two RIC men stood guard over the house on the hill around the clock, costing the taxpayer £2,000 a year. The documents relate that Killarney House had been shut up in November 1880 and the train of labourers dismissed, following a threat against Lord Kenmare's life, but the trustees now insisted on further economies and, in the end, Lord and Lady Kenmare had to close even their London house in Grosvenor Place and go to live on the Isle of Wight.

The marriage of Kenmare's son and heir, Lord Castlerosse, to the Hon. Elizabeth Baring of the banking dynasty in 1887 brought, according to the Kenmare Papers, 'a gratifyingly large marriage portion of nearly £16,000'. (Lord Castlerosse was the title reserved for the eldest Kenmare son during the tenure of each earl.) Life at Killarney House appears to have resumed a more stable rhythm in the tenure of this couple and their children, a new generation growing up in more settled times. Peace was restored at the end of the Land Wars and Kerry experienced a period of stability between 1890 and 1916.

An invaluable glimpse of the family's domestic life is given by Joseph O'Connor in *Hostage to Fortune*. O'Connor was engaged by Lord Kenmare in November 1899 as a tutor for his grandson, Dermot. He recalled being greeted by an English butler on his first visit and 'the silence of our movement on the deep carpets and the vista of long corridors reaching into the warm, hushed house'. Lady Castlerosse presided over the supper table, around which sat four of her children, Dorothy, Cicely, Dermot and Gerald, ranging in age from seven to fourteen years.

O'Connor describes her as 'strikingly handsome – the perfect model from the Madonna'. The following anecdote conveys the homeliness of the family unit set within the vast house:

> The moment their mother took her eyes off them, they made a concerted grab for the sliced fruit cake in the centre of the table. She swooped into instant action. She slapped the outstretched hands, rat-tat-tat, swept Gerald, the youngest marauder, off his chair and imprisoned him between her knees to keep him from climbing on to the table for his share of the loot.

Much of the passage deals with the impish Dermot (whose formal name was Maurice), 'a grand kid, full of surprises and keen as mustard'. The fate of the mischievous youngster is revealed in the chapter's two final lines: 'Dermot grew up to six feet of radiant masculinity, joined a regiment of Guards and paid his scot [*sic*] of the cost of empire with his young life in the retreat from Mons. And now, the empire for which he died is vanished.' Vanished too is the sumptuous mansion in which the young boy had played in 1899.

It was reduced to a smouldering pile of ashes and roofless, blackened walls in a fire that broke out between 4 and 5 a.m.

on Sunday 31 August 1913. A brief report in *The Kerryman* of Saturday 6 September stated, 'The fire appears to have originated in a room of the top floor of the right wing, and was first noticed by a male servant, who reported the outbreak to Lord Castlerosse and Lord Kenmare at 5 o'clock.' The report goes on to say that the private water supply was 'very indifferent' and that the hose fittings of Killarney Urban Council would not comply with the mansion's private supply fittings. Servants and locals rushed to the scene and helped to save valuable works of art, including family portraits, plate, light furniture, books, and valuable works of foreign artists, but furniture, tapestries, china, marbles and a masterpiece by the English artist and architect Inigo Jones were all burnt. The *Kerryman* report appears to have been written on the day of the fire but published the following week, and the unidentified journalist captures the drama of the blaze in these words: 'The chapel, forming the end of the eastern wing, remains intact, and the western wing, forming the servants' apartments, is counted safe, though the flames are still raging.'

On Saturday 6 September 1913, *The Killarney Echo* lamented that, 'The destruction by fire of the family seat of the Kenmare family has removed from the list of palatial halls of the Kingdom such a one as has ranked almost amongst the Royal residence for beauty of design.' The report related that, on the previous Monday, the newspaper's 'representative' was shown over the ruins by the Hon. Dermot Browne and was accorded an interview with Lord Castlerosse. Both looked on the burning of their lovely home 'quite philosophically, each gentlemen remarking that it was the fortunes of war'. The report describes the sight in the centre of the library floor of:

... a great tangle of ironwork, made of gas piping, the pipes of the heating apparatus and the melted and burned up metal work of several bedsteads, this wreckage having come from the top of the house and fallen from floor to floor as storey after storey caught alight and burned its way downwards.

The newspaper attributed the cause of the fire to 'an overheated flue' in the top of the house and quoted the amount of timber used in the construction of the house as a 'contributory factor'. It said the floors and stairs were 'simply saturated' over the years with floor polish, which was in itself an 'inflammatory material', and continued: 'The roar of the flames from the consuming wood was deafening, then the thunder of the falling floors, the fierce heat from the tongue of flame over a hundred yards high.'

The fire was a news event that travelled far. A New Zealand paper, the *Wairarapa Daily Times*, on 28 October 1913, incorrectly gave the date of the blaze as Sunday 6 September, and quoted 'interesting particulars' from *Lloyd's Weekly*. It reported that within twenty minutes of the alarm being raised at 'five o'clock', a large part of the right wing was 'involved'. By 'eight o'clock' the flames, shooting to a height of 60 feet, had obtained complete mastery of almost the entire premises. The report continued:

Everything possible was done to fight the fire but, before night the magnificent house, known to tourists the world over as one of the sights of Kilarney [*sic*], was a mass of ruins. Only the servants' quarters, a one-storey wing, was saved. The eastern wing, in which the chapel was situated, was the last to become ignited. Strenuous efforts were made throughout Sunday [*sic*] to save the chapel, but owing to inflammable pitch-pine floors, in which felting was inserted, these proved fruitless.

Among the 'priceless works' listed as being in the chapel were Italian marbles, an altar of Mexican onyx by Andre, and a reredos of Sicilian inlaid marbles. The report continued:

Very little of the furniture of the mansion was saved, except light articles, it being impossible to get the large pieces through the windows, while the risk of being trapped by the fire in the corridors rendered it unsafe for anyone to travel any distances through the house.

The newspaper also noted that Lord Kenmare, Viscount Castlerosse, the Hon. Dermot, Hon. Gerald and Lady Dorothy Browne took part in the work of salvage, and some family portraits and a few of the portable art treasures were brought out on the lawn. The interior description included that of the 'oak-panelled grand staircase which led up and out of the hall to the galleries, wainscotted in white carved wood, inlet [*sic*] with pictures'. Off the galleries opened the principal bedrooms, each of which had a view of 'the most perfect scenery in Ireland'.

It seems as if some of the Brownes, who were rendered 'homeless' by the fire, found 'lodgings' with the Vincents of Muckross House for a short time afterwards. In the Vincent visitor book for 1913, 'Kenmare' appears to have stayed at Muckross House from 31 August until 11 September. His son

Gerald was there from 31 August until 22 September. Another son, 'Castlerosse', was also there, but there are no dates for his stay.

The stables of the original Kenmare House near the town centre were converted into a residence following the fire. This house was known as Kenmare House, like the original, but is now called Killarney House. According to the Kenmare Papers, Lord Kenmare and his wife did not live there much, residing instead in London or in Hertfordshire (and legally giving up their Irish residency altogether in 1936).

Traces of the garden walls and terraces of the doomed mansion are still visible in the grounds of Knockreer House, built by descendants of the Brownes on a section of the original site. Knockreer House is now used as an environmental education centre. A mosaic, salvaged from the mansion's church, is on display in St Mary's cathedral beside the sacristy to the rear of the building.

Killarney's Old Order

The head gardener's house on the Kenmare Estate in Killarney was set at the edge of six acres of orchard bordered by Countess Road on one side and Muckross Road on the other. An underground tunnel linking the orchard to the estate proper inside the Golden Gates still exists today. When Michael Leane's father bought the gardener's house in 1941, the old order was slipping away, and the Kenmare era, which had defined Killarney for so long, was drawing to a close. Michael, my guide in my home town, related how the orchard was sold in plots of three-quarters of an acre, mostly to business people in College Street. During the war years the glasshouses were dismantled and the glass sold; the largest of these was donated to Muckross Gardens by Peter Malone, who had bought one of the sites.

Around this time the estate's Deer Park on the eastern side of the town was also sold. The name Deerpark is still used in sections of this area where remnants of the great wall enclosing the deer herds can still be seen in parts. Part of Lord Kenmare's stables has also survived in private ownership there. Michael explained that Woodlawn, a residential area covered with several housing estates from the 1960s onwards, was once owned by the Kenmares. The road running through it was private, and there were gates at either end. Woodlawn House, which stood in the green area of the estate, Woodlawn Park, is scarcely remembered today.

If you take as your starting point the Golden Gates located just minutes' walk from the jarvey rank, the orchard would have been across the road from you; portions of the 12-foot-high wall that surrounded it can be seen to the right of Countess Road and on Muckross Drive, a residential avenue running to the side of the former Leane family home, which is now a shop.

The Kenmare estate supplied milk to the town. Michael Leane's father, who was born in 1888, told stories of how in summertime the cows were milked out in the open. 'There was a big strike after World War One and the cows weren't milked,' Michael said. 'They closed down the milk business after that.'

Walking towards the town you will pass a large Celtic cross, a monument to the members of the Royal Munster Fusiliers who died in Burma, South Africa and West Africa between 1881 and 1902. To the left of the cross is a smaller memorial to the men of Killarney and beyond who served in the First World War. At its unveiling on 24 September 2009, President Mary McAleese said that many had come back 'disabled in mind and body'. Some of the soldiers were from the laneways of Killarney and poverty had driven them to enlist. George Taylor, who died in Flanders at the age of eighteen, was a son of Walter Taylor, Barry's Lane, Killarney. Walter, a sergeant major who had survived some twenty battles in India and Asia, returned home to work as a coachman at Muckross House.

As you turn right into East Avenue Road, there is an arched laneway directly across the road beside the International Hotel. Officially called Brewery Lane, it was 'Paddy's Lane' to generations because of Paddy Looney's sweetshop. Pride of place behind the counter was given to the green and gold top hat which Paddy proudly wore to countless All-Ireland finals.

In the 1960s two tall pairs of gates and pillars still stood at both entrances to the East Avenue Road, then called the Railway Road and privately owned. Michael remembers when a rope was tied across the gates once a year to assert ownership and locals had to ask permission to go through.

Killarney's modern cinema succeeded an earlier cinema, 'The Casino', which was started by a local company, including

Thomas G. Cooper, who took it over. A pioneer in the world of film, Thomas G. shot Ireland's first indigenous sound feature film, *The Dawn*, in 1934 and 1935. The East Avenue Hall, which originally stood on the site, boasted a maple-sprung dance floor. Lanterns hung in the trees to guide guests from the Great Southern Hotel down the pathway to the dances. The Great Southern Hotel, now called the Malton, was built in 1854 to serve the railway on a site that had been the gardens of the Countess of Kenmare. Her house stood on the present Countess Road, which is named after her. Again, up until the 1960s, a great pair of iron gates still hung on an entrance opening onto this road.

A stained-glass window by Harry Clarke and an extensive garden are just two reasons for visiting the Franciscan friary. In the side porch there is a simple holy-water font, which originated in the abbey on Innisfallen Island (well worth the traditional boat trip), and part of the skull of the Franciscan martyr Fr Francis O'Sullivan. Martyrs' Hill, where poets, patriots and priests were hanged in the 1600s, was located in the vicinity of the church.

Beside the friary and fronting Lewis Road is a hall called the *Áras Phádraig*. This was the original location of Killarney's RIC barracks, which, according to local historian Donal J. O'Sullivan, was partially burnt in August 1922 during the Irish Civil War. It is not known when it was demolished. Few people in Killarney today even know of its existence, but Joseph O'Connor has left us with an anecdote about 'Jack the Divil', Killarney's head constable in the early 1900s.

The O'Connors were living in at 47 High Street, where Jack

C. O'Shea's bar is today, when the house of their neighbour, Paud Fada, took fire on the last night of 1906. When the fire had eventually been put out, Joseph threw the bar open to his friends in the small hours of the morning. The bar was just about 'stone-dry' at 5 a.m. when Jack the Divil appeared on the scene with his men. 'His hard cold eyes ran over the relaxed warriors he had caught drunk on the licensed premises after closing time,' O'Connor wrote. Despite the excuse of the firefighting, thirty-two men were summoned to appear at the petty sessions.

One of the great landmarks of College Square was the Glebe Hotel, which was screened by a line of mature lime trees at the front and had an enormous garden to the rear. A fine magnolia tree growing beside the front porch was believed to be well over 100 years old. Originally a Church of Ireland residence, the building was leased by Archibald Graham in 1892 and run as a hotel by him until 1945 when Thomas G. Cooper took it over. Archibald Graham was the son of a Glasgow plumber who worked on the construction of Killarney House at Knockreer. A thriving business for years, the Glebe was derelict when it burnt to the ground in a fire that began late on the night of Sunday 24 January 1988.

Henn Street, or the 'Narrow Street', was the street of my childhood. The nearby Glebe Place and the laneways running off it had enough characters to people a collection of Chekhov short stories. There were three harnessmakers working in these lanes when I was growing up: John O'Grady, Jack O'Sullivan-Howard and Jerry Kelliher.

There were various explanations for the name Henn; it was attributed variously to an English military officer, an old family of solicitors and a Bianconi coach driver. Take your pick. A plebiscite to change the names of the main streets to those of the Easter 1916 Rising leaders in time for the anniversary celebrations in 1966 failed. This prompted an independent councillor, Denis Hussey from High Street, to declare, 'The people of Killarney have put their pockets before their nationalism.' But Henn Street did change, in around 1967, to Plunkett Street, in honour of the patriot Joseph Mary Plunkett who was executed in 1916.

Main Street was the centre for most of the major shops in town: the Emporium, Hilliard's, Reidy's, M. D. O'Shea's, Maher's and Curran's. The Emporium was owned by the O'Sullivan family, who were very active in politics. John Marcus O'Sullivan (1881–1948) was appointed Minister for Education in 1926. Behind the Town Hall on Main Street is St Mary's Well, a place of pilgrimage since 1302. The two big holy days at the well were 25 March, the Feast of the Annunciation, and 15 August, the Feast of the Assumption of Our Lady into Heaven. As with the custom with other holy wells, there were characters who offered to say the prayers or 'do the rounds' for pilgrims in return for a few pence.

Michael revealed that New Street has an unusual claim to fame in that the author, Abraham 'Bram' Stoker (1847–1912), who created Dracula, lived there when he worked in Killarney as an inspector of petty sessions, which were the equivalent of the district courts. The building in which he stayed stood close to where Dunnes Stores is now located.

Killarney's original parish church, which preceded St Mary's cathedral, was located in Upper New Street, and a little of the original stonework can be seen up high to the right of the archway opening into Chapel Lane. The Bishop's House was established in New Street in 1775 by Bishop Moylan. Tarrant's Coachbuilders of New Street built up a considerable export business for traps, sidecars and horse coaches of all types. In 1966 William Tarrant exported a trap and a full set of harness to Kansas City where it went on display at the American Royal horse show. He also sent a trap to Honolulu to a client named O'Sullivan.

At the very end of New Street, West End House was once a school of housekeeping set up by Lady Kenmare. Michael Leane remembers the laundry instructress, a Mrs Crane, who lived in the little tower house beside the Gleneagle Hotel with her husband, who was retired from the Australian police. She was an aunt of the Taoiseach, Jack Lynch, who used to holiday at the little house.

When Michael was walking to school through High Street, the tattoo of the anvil rang out from three forges, all owned by smiths called O'Shea. Jimmy O'Shea worked with his son. An artist with metal, Jimmy wrought gates, fixed farm implements, shod horses and made his own tools. One of his iron gates, embellished with a rose pattern, survives in the farmyard of the current Killarney House. Daniel O'Shea and his wife Cathryn lived at 49 High Street. They had twin sons, born on 14 November 1899. Daniel, born last, became a Franciscan priest. Michael (better known as Mackey), the firstborn, became one of the town's most successful entrepreneurs, building up M. D. O'Shea's & Sons from the humble beginnings of a donkey and car. One story goes that two of Mackey's employees had delivered goods to Cork city and were going for a quick pint when they saw Fr Daniel coming down the street in his Franciscan robes. 'Cripes, wouldn't he do anything to keep an eye on us,' the driver muttered, mistaking the priest for his boss.

The third smith, Frank O'Shea, operated a forge set back from the street on an incline close to where Foley's Restaurant is today.

No. 15 High Street was the location of Counihan's Travel Agency, which was started as a shipping agency by Cornelius Counihan in the 1860s. Starting out, he served as publican, grocer and shipping agent all in one but, in time, specialised solely in travel. Counihan's became the premier religious travel company in Ireland.

Killarney's first Methodist church was located behind No. 29 High Street, as was *An Dún*, a hall used for *céilidh* nights and as a meeting place for the Gaelic League and the Killarney Pipers.

A Strange Twist of Fate

A first-hand account of the death at the age of twenty-six of Fr Donal O'Sullivan from Killarney, while serving as an army chaplain at the Somme during the First World War, survived through a strange twist of fate. Fr O'Sullivan was anointing an English soldier at a crossroads in Aveluy on 5 July 1916 when a shell exploded, killing him instantly. However, the injured soldier survived and travelled to Killarney to meet the mother of the man who died while tending to him.

The young chaplain's nephew, Billy D. F. O'Sullivan, has been entrusted with his belongings, including the rosary beads that were in his pocket when he died and a piece of wood from a rifle case with his name engraved on it. The diary kept by the young army chaplain was also returned to his homeplace. Brief entries such as the following convey the horrors of the war. 'Distributed to the wounded. Went to see Taylor. He has lost both feet.' Two days later, he records, 'Poor Taylor died'.

Born in 1890 to Donal and Hannah O'Sullivan, who lived in the Black Valley before moving into Killarney, Fr Donal was ordained in 1914 and taught in St Brendan's Seminary until he joined the Royal Army Chaplains' Department. The bishop of the day, Dr Mangan, felt that so many Killarney men had joined the forces that someone should go with them to care for their spiritual needs. Fr Donal volunteered at once. On the battle front he did not limit his care to Irish soldiers or to Catholics alone.

Several family members have visited his grave in France. To this day, his memory is very much alive in the family. 'It's funny, he's always been in the mind of the family,' Billy O'Sullivan said. 'Even in the new generations.'

McCormack's Crubeens

Before I went to the table I asked the old butler what I would call the crubeens. He was an Englishman and he said, 'Pigs' trotters, my boy.'

So I went up to John McCormack and said, 'Pigs' trotters, sir.'

'You're a nice bloody Irishman with your pigs' trotters,' McCormack replied.

'Crubeens, sir,' I said.

'That's better,' the tenor declared, catching one and throwing it across the table, hitting the Chief Justice of the United States square in the chest while telling him, 'Here judge, have a crubeen.'

Jack O'Shea was in his eighties in the early 1980s when he related the above anecdote to me at his home on Mangerton Road, Muckross, where he lived with his sisters, Minnie and Peggy. Jack had been a waiter in Muckross House when John McCormack and his wife Lily were guests there in 1924. The American Bar Convention was holding a meeting in Killarney, and McCormack had been invited to sing for them. Following the performance, the group was invited back to Muckross for a late supper. Arthur Vincent, owner of the house, liked to show off indigenous Irish food, hence the young waiter's dilemma over the crubeens.

Jack, who had started work on the estate at the age of fifteen, served as farm man, waiter, hall porter and, eventually, valet to Arthur Vincent. He recalled that McCormack was always in good humour but that 'he was a wild devil when he had a few drinks in him'. Jack enjoyed a unique place in the affections of the Vincent family. Arthur Vincent's son Billy described him as 'the first person I remember in my life'.

Arthur Vincent, a Clare man, was a barrister on the Munster circuit before joining the judicial service of the British Foreign Office and serving as an assistant judge in overseas posts in Africa and Asia in the early 1900s. He married Maud Bourn, a Californian heiress, in 1910. The couple met in 1906 on board an ocean liner when he was coming home on leave. Vincent also served in Seanad Éireann.

Jack O'Shea travelled to California six times with the Vincents. Once, he drove from San Francisco to Vancouver with Arthur Vincent. He visited the two goldmines owned by the Bourns: the Empire Mine and the Star Mine in Spring Valley near Nevada County. He was shown a 'cake of gold' measuring 18 inches by 6 inches and was told that it was there for the taking by anyone who could lift it. 'I tried, but not a hope,' he said. He could have gone down a mine, but he 'wouldn't chance it'.

William Bourn bought Muckross House as a belated wedding present for his daughter and son-in-law who were honeymooning in the Muckross Hotel when they discovered Lord Ardilaun had put it up for sale. The couple's first child, Elizabeth Rose, was born in 1915. Billy was born in 1919. Elizabeth had a roomful of toys but she had just one favourite among them all. 'It was an old teddy-bear that got battered and worn,' Jack recalled. 'The maid sewed in a shoe button when the eye fell out. She would have given away all she had for that one toy.' Billy Vincent had a bulldog called 'Sergeant Buzz Fuzz' who was the gentlest dog imaginable but looked ferocious.

Muckross House was organised along the lines of a typical English country home. The servants were always a mixture of Irish and English until the Irish Civil War broke out and the English stopped coming. Rosa Lewis, one of the kitchen maids, became a favourite of Edward VII when she returned to England and went on to own the Cavendish Hotel. Lighting was restricted to candles and paraffin lamps. Jack recalled the Muckross winters as 'dreary'. There were open fires in nearly all the rooms. Arthur Vincent was a 'very good farmer' who utilised all the arable land very well and kept a big herd of traditional Kerry cows. All the workers were provided with housing.

The family visited France for three or four months at a time. Jack travelled to Paris, Cannes and Monte Carlo with them. Arthur Vincent always wanted to be back for the shooting and the fishing. The Vincents entertained politicians, artists and friends in their home. Their social circle included many Americans because of their ties with the USA. The visitors' book includes a poem by W. B. Yeats, who was a friend of Maud Bourn and visited the house several times. Jack remembered him as a 'quiet, distant man'.

William Bourn provided an income for the upkeep of the estate. In 1928 Maud developed pneumonia on an Atlantic crossing and died in a New York hospital. Her husband lived on at Muckross for four years after her death. Jack O'Shea had the following take on why the estate was eventually donated to the Irish state to become the Bourn Vincent Memorial and the nucleus of Killarney National Park: 'The big crash came in America and old Bourn thought he was broke. He cut off all the incomes for the estate. Vincent had not the money to keep it and he loved it too much to sell it. So, he handed it over to the state in 1932.' Elizabeth Rose and Billy were sent to school in England. Their father moved to France, where he remarried, but he returned to Killarney regularly, staying in the Great Southern Hotel and the Lake Hotel. He spent the war years in the Muckross Hotel.

Jack O'Shea, who lived a long life, held a very special place in the affections of the Muckross community. He was at the heart of the Muckross Rowing Club, from his youth as an oarsman right through to his days as a cox. He was also a stalwart member of Legion Football Club in Killarney.

Billy Vincent

A rthur William Bourn Vincent, born on 16 July 1919 and known in Killarney simply as Billy Vincent, was the son of the last private owners of Muckross House. His early childhood was divided between summertime in Muckross, Christmas in Cannes and regular liner crossings to America, where his mother's millionaire family owned two goldmines, a water company and substantial shares in oil and the railways. As a little boy, he would wake in the nursery in Muckross House and go next door to his mother, Maud, in her bedroom overlooking the picturesque Dundag Bay.

'She was a very vibrant person,' he recalled. 'She was very small but she was very vibrant, very intelligent and really a live wire. And she was amusing.' The pattern of life changed significantly in 1921 when Maud's father, William Bowers Bourn, suffered a stroke at his home, Filoli, near San Francisco. The young family was summoned to come immediately. Because the grandfather continued to suffer from strokes, the Vincents spent alternate years in Muckross and Filoli throughout the 1920s.

They had spent Christmas 1928 in Cannes and were returning to Muckross via Paris on 29 January when Billy's grandmother, Agnes, 'a worrier', cabled them to come again. It was to be a voyage with fatal consequences, as he related: 'So, off we went to San Francisco at a moment's notice. We had bad cabins on *The Majestic*. It was terribly cold, terrible weather. My mother caught pneumonia.' About six days after the liner berthed in New York, the vibrant young mother died at the age of forty-four. Billy was nine and a half years old, and his sister, Elizabeth Rose, was fourteen.

When I interviewed him in Killarney seventy years later, in 1998, he chuckled at first as he said, 'She died but of course my grandfather outlived everybody, including my grandmother.' But then there was a pause, and he added sombrely, 'But she was an only child and it really upset him.' The family was staying with Billy's godmother, Mrs Whitelaw Reid, on Madison Avenue when his father broke the news of his mother's death. I asked him if her death had a deep effect on the rest of his child-hood. 'Yes,' he replied simply.

The lonesome winter journey continued by train across the vast continent with the coffin of Mrs Vincent borne in a private rail car attached to the back of the railway express. The breaking of the journey in Chicago on 14 February 1928 was a memorable one for the nine-year-old boy; the day went down in American history as the Valentine Day Massacre. 'As we were driving up to the hotel, the sirens were going and the police were in every direction,' he said. The cause of the furore was all-out gangland war by Al Capone on an opposing gang of mobsters.

The family returned to Muckross the following October, but the halcyon days had died with Maud Bourn Vincent in New York. Billy was sent to school in Rugby near England, but he caught rheumatic fever after a year; the illness was to dog most of his teenage years. He spent two years at home in Muckross, either in bed or in a wheelchair. He had a private nurse and a tutor.

After the death of his mother, the next big upheaval in his life was ushered in by the Wall Street Crash in 1929. The family's finances were dependent on William Bowers Bourn, who had never really recovered from the death of his daughter. Billy explained the signing over of Muckross House and the 11,000-acre estate to the Irish state in this way:

> All the money came from him, you see. He was ill, in bed or a wheelchair all the time, and he was very disappointed after my mother died. He wanted to clear everything up so he sold the goldmine for a pittance in 1929. He had already sold Spring Valley,

the water company to the city (San Francisco). He wanted to get rid of everything, but he didn't want to sell Muckross, nor did my father. They thought it was such a beautiful place and they were acquainted with the national parks in California. They thought it was a perfect place to be a national park and they persuaded the government to accept it as such.

When he was told at the age of twelve years that the family was leaving Muckross for good, he was 'absolutely broken-hearted'. The nursery toys were donated to a local orphanage. Years later he would often meet people who told him they had played with his toys.

After the break with Muckross, the family was 'constantly moving'. When Billy's father remarried, he settled in Monte Carlo. Billy got on very well with his stepmother, who was much younger than his father and 'full of life and humour'.

The Muckross estate remained in limbo for some time after it was donated in 1932. Arthur Vincent was very disappointed at the lack of action and did not live to see the situation righted. According to Billy, he said, 'I should never have given it over. They'll never do anything with it.' With no mean amount of prodding from Billy Vincent, the government did eventually move to establish the national park.

Billy went on to lead a varied life, serving with the Irish Guards in the Second World War, helping to build a company into the second-largest helicopter business in the world and working in oil exploration and property development. A Mexican-based chocolate factory was one of his less successful enterprises. As a former president and chairman of the

American Irish Foundation, he channelled substantial funding to Irish-driven projects.

Monaco became home for Billy and his wife Elizabeth; the couple had been married sixty-three years at the time of his death, at the age of ninety-three, on 18 October 2012. He spent three months at his Killarney home every summer up to 1999. When I met him in 1998, he had made the journey overland in his fifteen-year-old Mercedes-Benz. The man whose family's generosity had made Killarney National Park a reality met with a refusal when he requested a site to build a home in the Muckross area. Instead, he built a house in Dromkerry, Fossa, on the opposite side of the town.

The sound of the wind soughing through the branches of a young oak tree and the melancholy notes of a slow air, 'Iníon An Fhaoit' ón nGleann', carried from the hilltop graveyard of Killegy in Muckross on 28 June 2013 as a final anthem to the late Billy Vincent as he was given over to his final resting place. His ashes had been brought from Monaco to be interred in a grave beside his father. For the son of a Clare-born judge and a Californian heiress, the wheel had come full circle in Muckross, his boyhood home and the place to where his heart returned no matter how widely he travelled.

The altruism of Arthur Vincent and the Bourn family ensured that the most beautiful lakeland and parkland in Killarney became a national preserve to be freely enjoyed by future generations. In the hands of other, less enlightened or more mercenary individuals, it could have become an exclusive playground for the rich and privileged.

If you have enjoyed the beauty of Killarney National Park,

raise a glass in memory of the generous souls of the Vincents and the Bourns. And while you are at it, remember too the American millionaire John McShain and his wife Mary, who chose to sell Killarney House and its estate to the state in 1978 for a price far below the market value on condition that the property was incorporated into Killarney National Park. Thanks to the philanthropic spirit of these two American families, there is virtually free and unlimited access to the lakeland paradise of Killarney.

Fighting Franco

Revd Robert Martin Hilliard, who was seriously wounded in 1937 at the battle of Jarama while fighting the fascists in the Spanish Civil War, had lived a full and eventful life by the time of his death, shortly after the battle, at the age of thirty-two. The Killarney man was a husband and father of four children and had been an Olympic boxer, a journalist, a Church of Ireland minister, an Irish republican and a Communist in his relatively short life. This list of labels is an indicator of the complex and passionate personality of this rebel of many causes, who was born into the tourist town's most prominent Protestant business family on 7 April 1904. At the time of Robert's birth the Hilliards were living at 79 New Street, but shortly afterwards his father bought the former Methodist manse or rector's residence, Moyeightragh, on Lewis Road.

The memory of the ardent republican was revived for many people in 1984 by a passing reference in a Christy Moore song, 'Viva La Quinta Brigada', which was released on his *Ride On* album and which pays tribute to the Irishmen who fought against the dictator, General Francisco Franco, in defence of the republic in the Spanish Civil War:

> Bob Hilliard was a Church of Ireland Pastor.
> From Killarney across the Pyrenees he came.
> From Derry came a brave young Christian Brother.
> And side by side they fought and died in Spain.

Some of us, whose attention fastened on those lines, were curious to learn more about the idealistic clergyman, later to become known as the 'Boxing Parson'. My research led me to his sister, Mary Shellard, the sole surviving member of the family of six brothers and sisters. Mary, Robert, Margery, Phyllis, Godfrey and Elsie were raised at Moyeightragh. Their father, also Robert, worked in the family haberdashery and leather business, R. Hilliard & Sons Ltd, of High Street, Killarney, which was founded in 1846 and was part of a partnership that took a lease of the Lake Hotel on the shores of Killarney's Lower Lake in 1897.

Mary, who was known in the family as 'Moll', remembered her younger brother as a 'very wild boy'. She recalled, 'Robert was always fighting, always on the side of the underdog. If any child was being bullied, Robert was in there defending them.' Much of Robert's boyhood was spent at his cousins' home, the Lake Hotel. Philip Hilliard, a cousin, recalled how Robert, at the height of one of his exploits, came crashing through a skylight in the hotel kitchen.

The fact that Robert left Moyeightragh at the age of ten to attend Cork Grammar School and, later, Mountjoy School in Dublin, meant that the family's memories of him were vague. Mary Shellard said, 'He had his colourful life away from the family.'

At the age of seventeen and enrolling at Trinity College, he gave his father's occupation as 'employed in a shop'. His nephew, Revd Stephen Hilliard, writing in 1988, said he was known to be someone who liked to walk on the wild side of life, rejecting all that was bland, all that was conventional. Revd Hilliard wrote:

On at least one occasion, while home on holidays from college, he fed the local IRA men downstairs in the kitchen of the family home in Killarney, leaving his nervous parents upstairs with strict instructions not to come down while he was entertaining these particular visitors. While he was at Trinity, Robert Hilliard played rugby, excelled as a boxer and was a founder member of the college's hurling club. He was Bantamweight Champion of Ireland for two years running, and in May 1931, took the Irish Featherweight Championship. He also represented Ireland in the 1924 Paris Olympics.

A member of Trinity's Thomas Davis Society, he was noted for his republican sympathies. Among the legends that have grown up around him is the one that he boasted of having voted for the anti-Treatyites in the 1922 election seventeen times before his breakfast. There are conflicting interpretations of why he left Trinity before he graduated, one being that his Olympic involvement distracted him from his studies, another that the college authorities disapproved of his republican sympathies.

In 1925 he married Rosemary Robins, and they settled near Surrey, where they had four children: Tim, Deirdre, Davnet and Kit. Deirdre (Davey) shared invaluable insights into the personality of her father with John Corcoran, a Limerick Institute of Technology lecturer in economics, who wrote about Robert Hilliard in the *Kerry Archaeological and Historical Society Journal*:

> I remember him as being a very loving father, a shoulder to ride on, a rescuer of small girls from the usual scrapes, smelling of tobacco and tweed, and who read or told grand stories at bedtime. We wanted him back, and were sure until that dreadful day that he would come.

The young father supported his family partly through a sortie into journalism and advertising. He is credited with having invented the slogan, 'Great Stuff this Bass'. A professed atheist at this stage, he returned to the Christian 'fold' through his involvement in Frank Buchman's Oxford Group, an evangelist sect of American origins. He felt that God was guiding him to return to Dublin and to enter the ordained ministry of the Church of Ireland. Back in Trinity, he found time to regain his boxing title and to edit the college magazine as well as to finish his degree. He was ordained in 1931 and given a curacy in the parish of Derriaghy outside Belfast. This Christian ministry was followed by another volte-face when he returned to London and joined the British Communist Party.

Mary Shellard saw her brother for the last time when he called to her Dublin home on the way to London. In late 1936 he was a member of the International Brigades in Spain, fighting with great distinction under Jock Cunningham and Frank Ryan in the 15th Brigade and mentioned in dispatches as Revd R. M. Hilliard.

Seamus Ware, author of *Irish Olympians*, quotes from an account of a training camp at Madrigueras in early 1937, describing the Killarney man as 'an ex-Anglican parson, a communist, a great drinker, one who had friends of all classes'. In the battle of Jarama, fought in February 1937, an estimated 7,000 republican soldiers, including Robert Hilliard, lost their lives. Despite the fact that he had embarked on a relationship with another woman, Robert remained close to his wife and family to the end. In a letter written to her on 1 January 1937, and made available by Deirdre Davey to John Corcoran, he wrote:

Teach the kids to stand for democracy. Thanks for the parcels, I expect they have been forwarded to me, but posts are held up a very long time and especially parcels. Do not worry too much about me. I expect I shall be quite safe. I think I am going to make quite a good soldier ... I still hate fighting but this time it has to be done, unless Fascism is beaten in Spain & in the world it means war and hell for our kids.

John Corcoran, who has visited the Jarama battlefield 200 miles south of Madrid, related how the republicans suffered heavy casualties on 12 February 1937 at what became known as 'Suicide Hill'.

Believed to have been seriously wounded while attempting to slow the advance of fascist tanks, Robert was taken to a republican military hospital for recuperation at Benicàssim, a Mediterranean coastal town. 'Unfortunately at Benicàssim his condition deteriorated, and he was transferred down the coast to the better equipped hospital at Castellón where he survived until 22 February,' Corcoran writes.

Richard Hilliard of Cahernane, Killarney, is a second cousin once removed of Robert Hilliard. (His father was a nephew of Robert's father.) Richard has a slightly different version of his ancestor's final days. The following anecdote, which he related to me in 2013, is disputed in *Black Sheep*, the RTÉ documentary on the clergyman, but I think it is worth recording nevertheless. While the Hilliards still ran their large department store on Killarney's Main Street, Richard received a visit from a Corkman, who claimed to have fought in Spain with Robert. He gave this account of his death:

> He told me that Robert had died in the hospital because a wall fell on his bed when Franco shelled the hospital. If that didn't happen, he might have come back to us. The man who told me that said he was in the next bed to him. He was absolutely positive he knew the man well. They were in it together. I have no reason to doubt him.

The Killarney man was buried with full military honours in a communal grave. John Corcoran has visited the cemetery, where the grave is unmarked. Robert Hilliard's name is inscribed on a family gravestone at Killegy, Muckross. The 'boxing parson' lived life with such an intensity that his story continues to captivate people today. When I interviewed Mary Shellard all those years ago, she said, 'He just won't die.'

War Heroine

A t the same time as Monsignor Hugh O'Flaherty was helping countless Jews and Allied personnel escape the clutches of the Nazis in occupied Rome, another Killarney native, Jane (Janie) McCarthy (1885–1965) was risking her life with members of the French Resistance in Paris to get similar people on the wanted lists safely out of the reach of the Gestapo. Janie was a Sorbonne graduate, who grew up in Killarney, a stone's throw from St Mary's cathedral at 74 New Street and was educated locally. As well as using her apartment as a safe haven for those on the run, the English-language teacher organised daring ruses to move people out of the city and across international borders. On one occasion she brought an American officer through a Gestapo inspection in the Paris Métro and passed him off as a deaf mute to disguise the fact that he could not speak French. The building in which Janie's top-floor apartment was located, 64 rue Sainte-Anne, in Paris's Second Arrondissement, is now partly given over to a Japanese restaurant.

While the involvement of Mons. O'Flaherty in saving an estimated 6,000 lives during the Second World War is now widely recognised in Kerry and beyond, thanks to a hard-working local committee, that day has yet to dawn for Janie McCarthy. Her wartime heroism was of such magnitude that, by the time she died in 1965, three countries had recognised her with the highest of honours. She was awarded a Legion d'Honneur (1950), a Croix de Guerre and a Croix de la Résistance in France. The USA honoured her with a Medal of Freedom and a citation from President Eisenhower. Her contribution to saving British personnel was recognised by a Tedder Certificate.

Janie left Killarney in 1910 to work as an au pair with a family in Brittany. She taught for fifteen years in Vannes and was a professor in a training college. She graduated from the Sorbonne with a degree in English and history. Her language classes in Paris attracted many pupils, including the children of royalty from Indochina. At the outbreak of the war in 1939 she exchanged her British passport for an Irish one to avoid being taken as a prisoner of war. She had many brushes with the authorities and many near-escapes. She escaped arrest on one occasion by missing an appointment with a Resistance member, Elisabeth Barbier, who was deported to Ravensbrück, a concentration camp for female political prisoners. Another time, she had to cancel a dinner invitation because of a language lesson; all the dinner guests were arrested by the Gestapo.

Her record of rescue missions was almost totally successful according to her obituary in *The Irish Times*: 'During the course of the whole war, she lost only one refugee – a French medical student – to a French double agent.'

An article in *The Kerryman* in December 1954 described her work and the regard in which she was held in France:

> For devotion to duty and service in the educational field during the First World War, she received the Palmes d'Academie in 1918, a very rare distinction for a foreigner to receive. She was teaching in Paris when the Germans occupied the city during the last war and within two months was a member of the resistance. She visited at least once a week the civilian camp at Saint Denis near Paris, the Military Hospital Val de Grace and the Sanatorium at Brevannes outside Paris. The money she earned, except just sufficient to pay for the bare necessities of life, she devoted to the welfare of the internees, young Frenchmen in hiding to escape working for the Germans or trying to get to England or the Maquis and Allied airmen who had been shot down. She engaged in many dangerous missions fetching parachutists into Paris to safe hideouts or guiding them from one refuge to another in the city.

The dangerous world she was moving in was a far cry from her sleepy Killarney birthplace where one of the few official records of her time there appears in the census of 1901. (The McCarthy family appears to have lived at both No. 74 and No. 15.) The census entry for the family at Lower New Street (House 15) reads as follows: Michael (fifty-four, caretaker), Margaret (fifty-two), children, Mary (twenty), Joseph (nineteen), Jane (sixteen), Elizabeth (eleven) and Frank (seven). Going by the census, Jane would have been twenty-five when she went to Brittany in 1910.

According to the parish records, the baptism took place on 20 January 1885 of Johanna Jane McCarthy of High Street; the year of birth tallies with that of the war heroine, as do the parents' names, Michael McCarthy and Margaret (Kelliher). The sponsors were Timothy McCarthy and Elizabeth Hayes, and the priest was Revd H. O'Kerin. Janie was, in fact, the ninth child in a family of fourteen children, four of whom did not survive to adulthood. The full list of Janie and her siblings is as follows: Timothy, Johanna, Jeremiah, Michael, Margaret Jane, Mary, Joseph, John, Johanna Jane, Margaret Josephine, Ellen, Elizabeth, Julia Mary and Francis.

Phil O'Connell, who grew up in New Street, had an aunt, Sally (Sara), who was good friends with Janie. Phil has a number of clear recollections of Janie's summer visits including the following:

Janie and Aunt Sally (Sara) RIP were good friends; in fact, Auntie was in charge of her house key and I did my piano practice in her house at number 74.

Janie came back each summer for a spell and brought some of her students to stay, some from Indochina and France as well. I became good friends with them all, such lovely people, as was Janie.

Janie would not settle at night until Sally went in to share a cigarette, nightcap and chat. Also, I can now hear Janie calling over the wall, 'Sara come and sit in the garden.'

One time, I recall Janie bringing Auntie a roll of the best French material to have a costume made. I can see Janie now, hair in a bun, smart French costume (suit) and of course all her medals on a ribbon, and speaking both in French and in English.

Sheila Mulcahy from Cloghane in West Kerry got to know Janie very well when she went to study in central France on a bursary in 1948 at the age of twenty. When Sheila landed at Orly Airport, Janie, an old friend of her mother's, was there to meet her. Janie was 'plump and unremarkable and always wore black'. But, for Sheila, her appearance was incidental. 'It was her personality that shone out. Talk about animation. She was a very outgoing person and good fun and great company.'

Sheila visited Janie's apartment only briefly on that first visit, but she was to get to know it extremely well on subsequent trips to Paris:

> She lived in a tiny flat on the top floor: one room was her sitting room and her bedroom; a small kitchenette adjoined it. She would have visitors – mostly young women who had been her pupils and who were quite glamorous Parisian women. They would be whispering in the kitchenette. I suspected that it was about their romances.

Sheila returned to France again from 1951 to 1954 to pursue her studies further. Accommodation was hard to find. At one stage Janie lent her flat to her while she was at home in Killarney. On another occasion she queued for hours to get Sheila a week of tickets to the Comédie Française – France's national theatre and the equivalent of the Abbey Theatre in Dublin, exclusively showing classic French and European theatre.

When Sheila ran short of money, Janie reached for a book on a shelf and took some franc notes from it. 'She was a lovable character,' Sheila said. 'She was very generous to me; she was so kind, she gave me the great gift of friendship.' Janie had an extraordinary circle of friends, among them Louise Schilman, who visited Killarney and who became a lifelong friend of Sheila's. Louise was from a Russian émigré family; her father was a tailor with one of the great houses of couture.

Sheila remembers Janie as a dedicated monarchist (in the French context) who used to say 'when we have our king back again'. She wore her war decorations discreetly but with pride. Although her command of French, including slang, was perfect, Sheila was surprised to note that Janie's accent was not quite native French. 'I would say in that in her generation students didn't think it necessary to speak as the French did.'

Paris-based Isadore Ryan researched the life of the patriotic Kerrywoman for his book, *Irish Paris*, but his search for further information on her is continuing. He learned that she joined the Resistance possibly through her friendship with Elisabeth Barbier, a former student of hers: 'As early as September 1940, Barbier, along with McCarthy, began to collate reports sent by a number of people on enemy activity for transmission to London. McCarthy also specialised in collecting information on rail movements in northern France.' Ryan describes her as a 'determined resister right from the start of the German occupation – a record few native French would have been able to emulate.'

Between 1940 and 1944, Janie worked successively for four different resistance networks. She features in several of the escape files written by the Allies. US airmen Bill Whitman and

Iva Fregette, who were forced to make a crash landing east of Paris, describe in their report that Janie came to visit them in their hideout in April 1943, along with Elisabeth Barbier, and supplied them with new papers to facilitate their journey by train from Paris to Bordeaux and from there to Saint-Jean-de-Luz on the Spanish border. Two other US airmen, who were confined to a hideout for several weeks, related that during those long weeks Janie paid them frequent visits and 'kept us laughing all the time'. In one of the files she is described as '45 years old, greying hair, plump'.

Although she was very ill in 1964, Janie continued to give language lessons from her bed until the end of June. Late in November of that year she was taken to the British Hospital in Levallois-Perret, where she died on 20 December 1964, aged seventy-nine. She was buried in the town cemetery there eight days later. The grave plot was leased for ten years to a Cornelius Healy but was not renewed and hence was leased out to another party in 1975. 'All the decorations she received, including the Croix de Guerre, didn't save her from being dug up ten years after her death and from her grave being leased out to somebody else,' Isadore Ryan concluded. 'Quite disgraceful, in my view.'

Louise Schilman told Sheila Mulcahy that she had been at Janie's funeral and remarked how strange it was to see thirty men 'weeping over her grave, who had never had a boyfriend'. A proposal was initiated in Killarney in late 2013 by Town Councillor Michael Gleeson to have a memorial created to the memory of the courageous Killarney woman; this may compensate to some degree for the lack of a burial place to visit. *Vive* Janie.

Famine Fire

At half past ten on the night of Friday 15 January 1850, the cry of 'Fire' was heard in College Street, Killarney. Within minutes, the smell of smoke was spreading through the town and people rushed frantically to the former college, a building which was being used as a female pauper hospital. An estimated 160 invalids were trapped in the burning building. Before the night was over, twenty-six children and three adults had lost their lives. But the irony of the terrible tragedy was that only two of the fatalities were caused by the fire; the majority of the deaths took place in a nearby building untouched by the flames.

By early 1850 there were eleven auxiliary workhouses in Killarney, crammed with the sick and starving Famine victims who had converged on the town in the hopes of saving their dwindling lives. One of the workhouses was located in a brewery located behind College Square, which gave its name to the nearby Brewery Lane. The female pauper hospital was located 500 yards further up College Street, most likely to the rear of the present Scott's Hotel. An eyewitness report in the *Tralee Chronicle* of Saturday 16 January 1850 opened with the words, 'I write to inform you of the melancholy occurrences that took place here last night – the burning of the female pauper hospital (formerly the college) and the falling of one of the floors in the auxiliary workhouse for children and grown girls.' The origin of the blaze was given as one of the rooms on the basement floor where a large quantity of straw had taken fire 'by some means, as yet unknown'.

People arriving on the scene witnessed the flames spreading rapidly to the upper floors and shutting off the lower staircase. Ladders were quickly procured and directed to the upper windows in a bid to rescue 'the helpless inmates – women and children – some stretched on the bed of sickness and others in the first stage of convalescence, now paralysed by fear'. In portions of the building, windows were being driven out with a sound like gunshots, and the fire was breaking through parts of the roof. Between sixty and eighty inmates, including a large number of 'poor children, perfectly naked', were saved by being passed down from the upper floors to people positioned at intervals on the ladders.

Even at this remove, the raw courage and heroism of the 'gentry and tradesmen' manning the ladders is infinitely touching; the bravery of 'that best of men', Dr Murphy, and two other individuals in particular was exceptional. *The Tralee Chronicle* delivers the drama of their rescue bids in detail:

> The fire had already reached the middle floor at this end but defying the danger, he [Dr Murphy] ascended the first ladder, forced his way through the upper window to the sick wards, followed by the Rev. Robert Hewson and the young Warren, and descended rapidly, bearing a naked, emaciated fellow creature on his arm. Five times did he ascend and descend the topmost storey with a like success, but at the imminent hazard of his life, the flames bursting through the windows of the middle floor and scorching both himself and the helpless objects of his kind solicitude.

The reporter relates that by 'such exertions' the building was cleared. By one o'clock, the roof had fallen in, and the entire premises presented 'an unbroken sheet of flame'. The casualties of the night were a child and a grown woman who had thrown herself from an upper window on the southern side.

But, sadly, the work of the volunteers could not prevent what was to unfold further down the street in the converted brewery building. When the sparks from the burning building were borne on the night breeze to the auxiliary workhouse, they caused the 'utmost alarm' among the women and children, as *The Chronicle* reported:

> No real grounds for alarm existed, but panic having seized them, they rushed, in their anxiety to escape, in large numbers on one of the weaker floors, which, giving way, twenty-five children and two grown females lost their lives. I am so sick at heart from the melancholy scenes I have witnessed.

The events of that night strike a chord in me because, 113 years later, in 1963, I was a child growing up on the other side of College Square, just yards away from where that old brewery must have stood. Our house caught fire at about the same time of night while my two brothers and myself (the three of us under four years of age) slept upstairs. Only for the heroism of local people, we too could have lost our lives. I remember especially my late neighbour, Haulie O'Donoghue, who braved the flames to find me in the smoke-filled bedroom and carried me to safety. God rest him and his family.

Goddess Country

O n 1 May every year, in a remote mountain townland, four miles from the village of Rathmore in east Kerry, all roads lead to 'the City'. The name might suggest a jaunt to the nearest metropolis of Cork city; not so. The city in question is an ancient religious site set at a height of 700 feet in the foothills of the Paps Mountains, a set of twin peaks looming above the Kerry and Cork border. Known as *Dhá Chích Danann* in Irish, the mountains, complete with stone cairns as nipples, represent the breasts of the ancient Goddess Danu or Anu. 'Arguably the best example we have of the female form monumentalised in western Europe,' according to archaeologist Michael Gibbons.

A goddess of fertility and prosperity, Danu was worshipped by the Tuatha Dé Danann, a legendary race said to have migrated to Ireland from Boeotia in Ancient Greece. Archaeologist Frank Coyne, in his study, *Islands in the Clouds*, explains that Danu was originally a European goddess, her name being incorporated, most famously, in the River Danube. 'It would appear that this river goddess had in Ireland become a land goddess, as Anu and Danu appear to be one and the same divinity,' he wrote.

Originally a pagan centre of worship, the City has always had strong associations with cattle and fertility; cattle were once herded from long distances to the site for a blessing and protection against disease. But the City met the fate of many pagan sites which were Christianised and, after some centuries, tamed. Its original title, *Cromlech Cathair Crobh Dearg*, is loosely translated as 'Red Claw's Mansion'. Red is associated with blood, death and sacrifice. According to Frank Coyne, *Crobh Dearg* or Red Claw, to whom the holy well at the City is dedicated, was one of three sister saints once revered in the area. The 'saints' who, he says, do not seem to appear in the Christian calendar are St Latieran, or Breast of Light, St Lasair, also known as *Crobh Dearg*, and St Iníon Buí, or Yellow Daughter. A holy well is dedicated to them and each is associated with a pagan feast day: Lasair with Imbolc on 1 February and the City at Shrone; Iníon Buí with Bealtaine on 1 May and the holy well in Dromtarriffe, County Cork, and Latieran with Lughnasa on 1 August and the holy well in Cullen, County Cork.

For Michael Gibbons this sisterhood of saints offers the best possible evidence of a link with the pre-Christian past at the site. 'The one location where we do appear to have some evidence for possible continuity is the City,' he said. 'The idea of a continuous link between modern mountain pilgrimage and the pagan past is a valid and active one here because of the place-name saints' association with pagan feast days.'

The Paps, Michael contends, represent key evidence of a pagan pilgrimage tradition. 'With the Paps we do have a Celtic deity we can be happy with,' he said. His endorsement of the pilgrimage tradition at the City lends weight to the claim that it is the oldest site of continuous religious worship in Europe. For locals the City is a place of pilgrimage and prayer, a place so obviously part of their heritage and the countryside that there is no need for directional signs to find it.

Revisiting the City in September 2013 after a gap of nearly a decade, with two friends and a visitor from the desert area of Las Vegas, we, the Kerry folk, were confident we would locate it without a problem at the end of our ten-mile drive on the N72 from Killarney. We passed through the village of Barraduff and continued on until we reached the right-hand turn signposted for Shrone. At Shrone National School, which was celebrating its 150th anniversary, we paused at the crossroads where there is a large information board about the City. Beside the board stood a brown sign pointing left: the only word discernible on its faded surface was *Slí*, meaning 'way' and sending us entirely out of our way on a narrow, winding road. The brown sign, we learned afterwards, was part of the Duhallow Trail.

Like most experiences of getting lost, it was not without its gifts. We eventually stopped at a house where an elderly lady told us that we were six miles from Millstreet in County Cork, and that we should have gone straight ahead at the school. We made some casual conversation about the narrow width of the road and she came out with a line of pure poetry: 'I do throw the holy water on myself going out the door the way the young fellows come lifting round the bends.'

When you make your journey, expect no signs for 'The City', other than the initial information board and two more boards directly in the vicinity of the site. Continue straight on at the crossroads near the school, down a dip, up again and, as they say in Kerry, 'hold going' until the road curves round to the left, rising again to the site, which has a ruined cottage with a rusting corrugated roof at its edge. From the crossroads to the City is a drive of about three minutes or so. There is no parking area, so find a space where you can at the grassy verge of the road.

An unmarked path through rushes and across a little stream will bring you to the entrance point beside the holy well, set just outside the encircling stone and earth wall. Incidentally, the ancient well now gurgles in an upright section of concrete pipe. Your feet are now touching the ancient soil of *Sliabh Luachra*, a cultural territory often described as being as much a state of mind as a place. The City is to *Sliabh Luachra* what Athens is to Greece.

If you were expecting a fully formed stone circumference wall similar to Staigue Fort near Castlecove on the Ring of Kerry, think again. Much of the original wall has been removed, but the circular formation of the original settlement is obvious. What you get here is a raw, unadulterated experience of a sacred landscape which has not been prettified or packaged into a tourist experience. Note the flat stones with the sign of the cross scored chalkily into the surface by pilgrims using sharp stones left lying beside them. If you choose to, use one of the stones to trace the sign of the cross and add your energy to that of generations stretching back into the mists of time.

The real authority on the City, local man Dan Cronin, confesses to coming to the art of writing in the autumn of his life, but the wait has done him – or us – no harm. His book, *In the Shadow of the Paps*, is informative and engaging. Dan, who first saw the light of day in a thatched farmhouse in Aunaskirtane, *Abha na Sceardán*, a townland taking its name from a fast-flowing noisy river, gleaned much of his knowledge from men whose stories were 'passed like torches' from generation to

generation through the tradition of the *seanchaí* or storyteller.
He writes:

> Petitions were made to the gods for fertility for man and beast, good
> return from the land, good crops and fodder. Even today, 4,000
> years later, several small offerings are placed on ledges near the ruins
> of pagan altars on the top of the Paps Mountains for the health of
> the family and of the cattle and for fertility. May is the significant
> month at the City because of its association with fertility in nature
> and the advent of summer.

Dan imagines the festivities of May Day or *Lá na Bealtaine* in
olden days as follows: 'The music of pipes and fiddles re-echoed
from the hills and valleys, and the lowing of cattle mingled
with the sweet music of the harp. Jesters and jugglers plied their
trade with everybody trying to make themselves heard.' Ale was
brewed there 'in plenty' with the result that, in the late 1800s,
the parish priest of Rathmore denounced the City from the
altar because of the 'libations'. According to Dan, as a result of
the Second World War restrictions everything fell away, apart
from the religious side of the May Day observances.

A painted plaster statue of Our Lady of the Wayside has
been erected close to the Megalithic altar in the enclosure, two
tides of tradition pulling against each other but maintaining
a common female connection to divinity. Between 1 and 12
May, people come to 'pay' the rounds, reciting Hail Marys and
Our Fathers as they circle the sacred site, and drink from the
bubbling holy well. Fr William Ferris, preaching at the City
on 1 May 1925 and quoted in Dan Cronin's book, said that

some of those who came to worship there spoke a language akin to modern Basque. He said it was a holy place even before Palestine became the Holy Land.

The City came close to having its own hospital in the 1950s. Dan relates how a bank in Massachusetts in the USA had contacted the then Health Authority in Kerry, enquiring on behalf of a client as to the feasibility of building a hospital in the area. The Health Authority turned down the offer from the anonymous benefactor, but the people of the area formed a committee and contacted the bank manager to say they would welcome a church. On 19 July 1954 the church of Our Lady of Succour was blessed and opened. The emigrant who had donated £80,000 turned out to be a local man, Tim Scannell, whose gravely ill mother had died on the road to Killarney while being transported there in a donkey and car.

While you are in the general area, Shrone Lake is worth seeing, as are the stained-glass windows in St Joseph's church in Rathmore, which translates as *An Ráth Mhór* or the 'big fort'. Rathmore is a village with a highly evolved social conscience, thanks chiefly to its Social Action Group, which has initiated numerous community projects since its inception in 1975. Of course, if your time is your own, you can always follow the *Slí* sign on a caprice and see to which goddess or ancient saint it will lead you: just watch out for any young fellows 'lifting round the bends'.

The Moving Bog

The Runaway Bog or, as it is better known in Kerry, the Moving Bog, was a natural disaster that claimed eight lives on 28 December 1896, when a thunderous wave of peat and water swept a family away as they lay sleeping in their home, little realising the menace that was bearing down on them. The disaster happened between 2 and 3 a.m. in the townland of Knocknageeha, which is at a height of about 750 feet and close to the Kerry and Cork border. The area is 12 miles east of Killarney and 1 mile from the village of Gneeveguilla. At the time, it was part of the Kenmare estate.

The family at the centre of the tragedy comprised Con Donnelly (forty-four), the steward of a nearby limestone quarry owned by Lord Kenmare; his wife, Johanna (thirty-eight), and their children, Daniel, Hannah, Humphrey, Katie, Margaret, James and Eliza (Lizzie), ranging in age from sixteen years to eighteen months. Thirteen-year-old Katie Donnelly, the sole survivor, had left home the previous afternoon to bring Christmas gifts to her grandmother in Mountcain, Knocknagree, which was located just across the border in County Cork. She was brought back the following morning, but her home had totally vanished; a sea of mud and chunks of bog deal covered the site.

The bog gushed cross-country until it reached two river systems and continued via them into Lough Lein 14 miles away in Killarney; a piece of one of the beds from the Donnelly cottage was found in the lake. The outpouring from the bog continued in fits and starts for about three days, covering acres of land and putting other residents in dread of sleeping in their homes at night.

Tom Joe O'Donoghue, a grandson of Katie Donnelly, lives beside the site of the disaster. 'It must have been some sight to look down and see that thing,' he said. 'To come back the following morning, wasn't that an awful attempt? Now, they would try to shelter someone from that. Funnily enough on the day that was in it – 28 December, it was the feast day of the Holy Innocents.'

The bodies of Katie's sisters Lizzie and Margaret and her brother James were never recovered, despite the courageous efforts of search parties wading waist-deep in freezing black water. 'There are three children still out there somewhere,' Tom Joe said. 'They had a baby in the cradle – Lizzie. When the floods subsided, the cradle was found jammed in a tree. The only ones to survive the tragedy that night were the dog and the duck. The dog ran and the duck could swim. My grandmother said she didn't want to see them at all. In a way, I suppose, they were taking the place of her family.'

Tom Joe and his family live at Knocknageeha, just a few yards up the road from the Moving Bog Memorial, which marks the exact site of the Donnelly home. He described the events of that fateful night as the story was handed down to him:

The bog came down from Coom Upper. They were on this side of the road and the bog was on the other side of the road. They call it the Moving Bog but it was actually ninety per cent water. If you have enough water in anything, it will flow. It will head for the fall. That's natural. The sound of it was frightening, they said. If you can imagine a small *glosha* (stream) in flood, you can imagine that – twenty metres high and it heading for Killarney as fast as it could.

The day was actually the Fourth of Christmas Fair, the fair day held in Killarney on 28 December, which was the fourth day of the Christmas season. There were people going down from Lacca to the fair when their horses stopped dead on the road. One man, Linehan from Mountcain (they called him the Champion), hopped out of the rail (cart) when he could not get the horse to go any farther. He was up to his knees in bog stuff.

When it was all after happening, it was asked and asked why they had not moved out when they had been warned several times. There was such vibration in that bog that the cups used to be rattling on the dresser. It was very volatile.

An expert committee was set up by the Royal Dublin Society to investigate the disaster through the first weekend of January 1897; poor drainage and an accumulation of water were among the eventual findings of the committee which used the term 'Runaway Bog'. The issue was still live enough on 25 April 1901 to exercise the mind of a Kerry MP, John Murphy, in the House of Commons. He asked the Chief Secretary of Ireland, George Wyndham, whether he had information showing that 'this disaster was primarily due to the fact that the landlord of the district never made any effort to effect a proper outlet for the surplus water in the bog.'

Tom Joe's grandmother told him that if the bog had followed the fall of ground into the Blackwater river on the Cork side of the border, the tragedy could have been even more devastating. 'I often heard my grandmother say that if it went the other side, it would have done the red "divil" in damage. There would have been up to half a dozen families carried on the Blackwater side.'

The material removed from the surface of a bog in preparation for cutting sods of turf is called 'stripping'. Large sods of stripping were carried overland in the torrent which eventually made its way into rivers, including the Owneycree, and blocked Barraduff Bridge, causing widespread flooding. Apart from the deaths of the Donnelly family, there was wholesale destruction of roads and farmland. 'It created havoc with the farmers down the river. There would be nice grassy inches and when that blasted thing poured over it, they lost a lot of land,' Tom Joe said.

One townland, Tooreenamult, was barely touched, he believes, because it was close to Lord Kenmare's quarry, which took the brunt of the force when the deluge poured into it, practically filling it. Afterwards, the quarrying operation had to be transferred to the opposite side of the road.

Gneeveguilla-born journalist and author Donal Hickey, who has researched the tragedy extensively for the *Sliabh Luachra Journal*, wrote that at about nightfall on the day before the bogslide, a heavy downpour commenced, driven by a south-easterly gale. Some time between 2 and 3 a.m. the following morning, the edge of the bog gave way, releasing a massive flood of peat and water. An eyewitness, John Riordan, reported seeing a 'moving mountain of fire' and hearing a noise like thunder. Experts later attributed the light to underground chemical disturbances causing a powerful phosphorescent glow.

Helpless before the force of the torrent, the Donnelly parents and children, their livestock and fragments of their house and furniture were swept down the valley. When Johanna Donnelly's body was found a mile and a half away from her home the day after the bog moved, those who discovered her said her face bore a very calm and peaceful expression as she lay there on the mud surface. Her husband's body was found near Annagh Bridge the same day. The body of the eldest son, Daniel, was found on Thursday 31 December in Tooreenamult, and Hannah's body was found at Scrahanfadda on 5 January. On 8 February, Humphrey's body was found, just a few miles outside Killarney in the Flesk river at Minish.

Because a number of roads were blocked by debris, their coffins had to be borne past the site of their home. A family story passed down to Tom Joe suggested that Katie's mother, Johanna, had a premonition of this. She returned home from visiting a neighbour's house one night and told her husband she had seen the 'strangest thing'. 'I am after meeting two big coffins and a lot of children's coffins going up the road,' she is reported to have said.

'How would they be going up the road, and where would they be going?' he replied, dismissing her fears.

The cruel fate of the family, who had lived their lives in relative obscurity, created waves as far away as London. A committee for the relief of distress was set up on 6 January 1897. A fund to compensate Katie Donnelly and other affected families received donations of £100 from local people and rose to £186. Queen Victoria's donation of £5 was criticised in the local nationalist paper, *The Kerry Sentinel*, for its paucity. Maybe this influenced

Katie Donnelly's politics. Her grandson remembers her as being a 'bit Republican-minded'; she had a full-sized portrait of Robert Emmett on the sitting-room wall. 'She said the disaster fund did no good,' he said. 'She used to be giving out about it.'

Katie was reared by her Knocknagree relatives and sent to school for a time at the Loreto Secondary School in Killarney. While working in Manchester, she met Paddy O'Donoghue from Ballaugh, Killarney. They eventually returned to Knocknageeha and built the house which still forms part of Tom Joe's own home. The couple accumulated 12 or 13 acres of 'pure raw bog'. They could have claimed a further 8 acres but Katie was short one shilling the day she went into Lord Kenmare's estate office in Killarney. 'The agent, Leonard, was going to give it to her but she needed the stamp,' Tom Joe said. 'She didn't have the shilling for it.'

Katie died on 17 October 1964, aged eighty-four. Her gravestone in the cemetery at Gneeveguilla bears the legend, 'Sole Survivor of the Moving Bog'. Her parents and siblings were laid to rest in Knocknacopple graveyard near Rathmore; no headstone marks their resting place, and the exact location of the family plot is unknown.

Bibliography

Barrett, J. J., *In the Name of the Game* (Dub Press, 1997)

Barrington, T. J., *Discovering Kerry* (Collins Press, 1999)

Bary, Valerie, *Houses of Kerry* (Ballinakella Press, 1994)

Byrne, Anne, 'Untangling the Medusa', in *Stars, Shells and Blue Bells: Women Scientists and Pioneers* (Women in Technology and Science, 1997)

Chenevix Trench, Charles, *The Great Dan: A Biography of Daniel O'Connell, The 'Liberator of Ireland'* (Triad Grafton Books, 1986)

Conlan, Fr Patrick, OFM, *Irish Franciscans in the Nineteenth Century* (forthcoming)

Corcoran, John, 'The Rev. Robert Martin Hilliard (1904–37)', *Kerry Archaeological and Historical Society Journal*, Series 2, Volume 5, 2005

Coyne, Frank, *Islands in the Clouds: An Upland Archaeological Study on Mountain Brandon and the Paps, County Kerry* (Kerry County Council in consultation with Aegis Archaeology Limited, 2006)

Cronin, Dan, *In the Shadow of the Paps* (Crede, Sliabh Luachra Heritage Group, 2001)

Dennehy, Emer A., 'Dorchadas gan Phian: The History of Ceallúnaigh in County Kerry', *Kerry Archaeological and Historical Society Journal*, Series 2, Volume 2, 2002

Dolan, Terence Patrick, *A Dictionary of Hiberno-English* (Gill & Macmillan, 2013)

Dwyer, T. Ryle, *Submarines in the Bog Holes: West Kerry's Experience of World War II* (The Kerryman, 1999)

Fitzmaurice, Gabriel, *In Praise of Football* (Mercier Press, 2009)

Flahive, Michael, *The Last Voyage of the Dronningen* (The Shannonside Journal, 1993)

Gaughan, Fr Anthony J., *Listowel and Its Environs* (Mercier Press, 1973)

Giblin, Fr Cathaldus, *Daniel O'Connell and the Irish Franciscans* (The Franciscan College Annual, Multyfarnham, 1950)

Goddard, Stanley Edward, *All Roads Lead to Kenmare* (Trafford Publishing, 2006)

Gourley, C. E., *They Walked beside the River Shannow* (The Kerryman, 1966)

Guerin, Michael, *The Lartigue, Listowel and Ballybunion Railway: World's Most Unique Monorailway and Its People, 1888 to the Present Day* (Lartigue Centenary Committee, 1988)

Hardiman, Adrian, 'The Doneraile Conspiracy', a lecture delivered at Derrynane House, County Kerry, on 7 September 2013 as part of the O'Connell Heritage Summer School

Healy, T. M., House of Commons Debate, 24 March 1887, vol. 312, c. 1434, http://hansard.millbanksystems.com/commons

Herbert, Dorothea, *Retrospections of Dorothea Herbert, 1770–1806* (Town House, 1988)

Hickey, Donal, 'The Life and Times of Katie Donnelly, Sole Survivor of the Moving Bog Disaster', *Journal of Cumann Luachra*, Vol. 9, August 1998

Hickey, Donal, 'The Night the Bog Moved', *Journal of Cumann Luachra*, Vol. 8, August 1986

Hilliard, Stephen, *The Boxing Parson* (Resource Spring, 1988)

Horner, Arnold, *Iveragh, Co. Kerry in 1811, Alexander Nimmo's Map for the Bog Commissioners, With Extracts from His Report and a Commentary by Arnold Horner* (Glen Maps, 2002)

Humphrys, Mark, 'Aghavallen Church, near Ballylongford', http://humphrysfamilytree.com/Blennerhassett/aghavallen.html, accessed 9 April 2014

Hussey, Samuel, *The Reminiscences of an Irish Land Agent* (Duckworth & Co., 1904)

Jackson, John Wyse, and Costello, Peter, *John Stanislaus Joyce: The*

Voluminous Life and Genius of James Joyce's Father (St. Martin's Press, 1997)

'Janie McCarthy, French Patriot from Kerry', *The Irish Times*, 2 January 1965

Joy, Breda, 'Billy Vincent: No Magic Circle Surrounds His Universal Experiences', *The Kerryman*, 4 September 1998

Joyce, P. W., *English as We Speak It In Ireland* (Wolfhound Press, 1910)

Keane, Fergal, 'So Much of Our Irish Past Is Snagged with Myth and Suppressed Memory', *The Independent*, 1 January 1999

Keane, John B., 'Listowel John B. Keane Talks About Tom Doodle', ListowelArcade, available on http://www.youtube.com/watch?v=EtMj8GDvmvE, accessed 9 April 2014

Kelleher, D. L., *Great Days with O'Connell* (The Talbot Press, 1929)

'Killarney Conflagration, Lord Kenmare's Mansion Destroyed by Fire', *The Kerryman*, 6 September 1913

'Killarney Conflagration, Nearly One Hundred Rooms Destroyed', *The Killarney Echo*, 6 September 1913

Knightly, John, 'Lixnaw and the Earls of Kerry', *Kerry Archaeological and Historical Society Journal*, Series 2, Volume 10, 2010

Locke, Peter, 'Mulchinock and the Rose of Tralee?', *Kerry's Eye*, August 2002

Looney, Fr Tom, *Dick Fitzgerald: King in a Kingdom of Kings* (Currach Press, 2008)

Lynch, Patrick J., *Tarbert: An Unfinished Biography* (Fitzsimons Printers, 2008)

McAuliffe, Bridget, *Uncovering Kerry: The Comprehensive Guide to the Best of Kerry* (Red Hen Publishing, 2006)

McCoole, Sinead, '*The Herberts of Muckross*', *Killarney History and Heritage* (The Collins Press, 2005), pp. 90–104

McDonagh, Marese, 'Why I Breached Irish Neutrality', *The Kerryman*, 21 September 1984

McElligott, Dr Richard, *Forging a Kingdom: The GAA in Kerry, 1884 to 1934* (Collins Press, 2013)

McKenna, Canon John, 'The French Revolution: The Dingle Connection', *The Kerry Journal*, 1989

McMorran, Russell, and Clare McMorran (drawings), *Tralee: A Short History and Guide to Tralee and Environs* (R. and C. McMorran, 1980)

Mulhall, Dan, 'King Dan and the German Prince: Daniel O'Connell's Meeting with Hermann von Pückler-Muskau, September 1828', Lecture, Derrynane House, 1 September 2012

Murphy, Junior, *Cahersiveen: The Town that Climbs the Mountain* (Clóbhuainn in Éirinn, 2009)

Nelligan, Pat, and Liam Higgins, *Dingle and Marie Antoinette* (FÁS Video, 2012)

Ó Concubhair, Pádraig, 'From Buck House to the House of Healing: Albinia Brodrick/Gobnait Ní Bhruadair', lecture delivered at Kerry County Library, 12 February 2013

O'Cleirigh, Nellie, *Valentia: A Different Irish Island* (Portobello Press, 1992)

O'Connor, Janet, *An Rábach of Cummeengeera: The Fact and the Theatre* (Lulu.com, 2012)

O'Connor, Joseph, *Hostage to Fortune* (Michael F. Moynihan Publishing Company, 1955)

Ó Faoláin, Seán, *King of the Beggars: A Life of Daniel O'Connell* (Poolbeg Press, 1980)

O'Hare, Patricia, *The Bourn Vincent Family of Muckross, Killarney History and Heritage* (Collins Press, 2000)

Ó Luanaigh, Fr Tomás B., 'Martyr Francis O'Sullivan: The Ardea Connection', *Tuosist 6000* (1999)

Ó Lubhaing, Bearnard, *Ventry Calling* (Mercier Press, 2005)

O'Mahony, Joe, *The Kingdom: Kerry Football, the Stuff of Champions* (Gill & Macmillan, 2010)

O'Rourke, Alan, *The North Kerry Line: A History of the Limerick–Tralee Railway and the Branches to Foynes and Fenit* (The Great Southern Trail, 2013)

O'Rourke, Kathleen, *Old Killarney* (The Kerryman, n.d., *c.* 1918)

Quinlan, Seán, *The Great Book of Kerry*, Volume 2 (Cló na Ríochta, 2008)

Reid, Thomas, *Travels in Ireland in the Year 1822* (London, 1823)

Ryan, Isadore, *Irish Paris: Stories of Famous and Infamous Irish People in Paris through the Centuries* (Blurb, 2012)

Schreibman, Susan, 'A Raid on the Inarticulate: The Poetry of Thomas McCreevy', *Kerry Magazine*, No. 5, 1994, pp. 23–4

Smith, Charles, *The Ancient and Present State of County Kerry* (Mercier Press, 1969)

Starken, Elizabeth, 'From the Boglands of Lyre We Came', *Duagh Parish Newsletter*, June 2006

Stoakley, T. E., *Sneem: The Knot in the Ring* (Sneem Tourism Association, 1986)

Villiers-Tuthill, Kathleen, *Alexander Nimmo and the Western District: Emerging Infrastructure in Pre-Famine Ireland* (Connemara Girl Publications, 2006)

Ware, Seamus, 'The Boxing Parson: Killed in the Battle of Rio Jarama (and the OCI Ex-President, on the Other Side in Spain)', *The Journal of Olympic History*, May 2002

Wells, Grace, 'The Coat', *Sunday Miscellany*, RTÉ Radio 1, August 2011

Young, Arthur, *A Tour in Ireland* (Blackstaff, 1983)

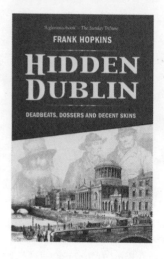

Hidden Dublin

Frank Hopkins

978 1 85635 591 9

Criminal incidents, accidents, whippings, beatings, jail escapes and hangings were all part of Dublin life in the eighteenth and nineteenth centuries. Actors, clergymen, scientists, politicians and rogues and rascals of every hue contributed to the hidden life of Ireland's capital. *Hidden Dublin* brings these events and characters, and more like them, to life in a riveting history of Dublin that you won't find in any schoolbook or guidebook.

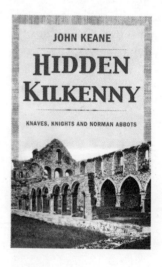

Hidden Kilkenny

John Keane

978 1 78117 157 8

Hidden Kilkenny delves into the colourful history of the city and county of Kilkenny, to explore the largely forgotten but fascinating stories of many of its hidden gems. From the thatched villages of South Kilkenny to the often overlooked treasures of Kilkenny city, the book explores castles, great houses, abbeys and tombs, and the characters who populated these places. John Keane skilfully brings the hidden past of Kilkenny to life.

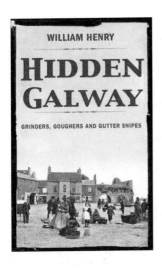

Hidden Galway

William Henry

978 1 85635 754 8

William Henry delves into the rich tapestry of Galway's past to reveal a totally new history of the city and county. There are accounts of disasters, chilling tales of execution and murder, and love stories. Bandits, highwaymen and smugglers are part of this hidden history, as are scientists and men and women of vision. *Hidden Galway* brings the history of Galway to life in a book that has something for everyone.

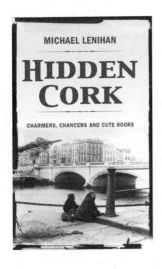

Hidden Cork

Michael Lenihan

978 1 85635 686 2

From quack doctor Baron Spolasco, to the outlaw Art Ó Laoighre, Cork has been home to some eccentric, wonderful and downright nasty people down through the centuries. In *Hidden Cork* Michael Lenihan delves into Cork's history to reveal some of its most bizarre events and strangest characters, opening the door on history, dumping the boring bits and bringing to life the flow of time through the streets of Cork.

MERCIER PRESS

IRISH PUBLISHER - IRISH STORY

We hope you enjoyed this book.

Since 1944, Mercier Press has published books that have been criti-
cally important to Irish life and culture.

Our website is the best place to find out more information about
Mercier, our books, authors, news and the best deals on a wide variety
of books. Mercier tracks the best prices for our books online and we
seek to offer the best value to our customers, offering free delivery
within Ireland.

A large selection of Mercier's new releases and backlist are also
available as ebooks. We have an ebook for everyone, with titles
available for the Amazon Kindle, Sony Reader, Kobo Reader,
Apple products and many more. Visit our website to find and
buy our ebooks.

Sign up on our website or complete and return the form below to
receive updates and special offers.

www.mercierpress.ie
www.facebook.com/mercier.press
www.twitter.com/irishpublisher

Name: _____

Email: _____

Address: _____

Mobile No.: _____

Mercier Press, Unit 3b, Oak House, Bessboro Rd, Blackrock, Cork, Ireland